GOOD SHELTER

*A Guide to Mobile, Modular, and
Prefabricated Houses, Including Domes*

GOOD SHELTER

*A Guide to Mobile, Modular, and
Prefabricated Houses, Including Domes*

Judith and Bernard Rabb

NYT

Quadrangle / The New York Times Book Co.

Designed by Tere LoPrete

Library of Congress Cataloging in Publication Data

Rabb, Judith, 1941–
  Good shelter.

  Bibliography: p.
  Includes index.
  1. Mobile homes. 2. Modular construction.
3. Prefabricated houses. I. Rabb, Bernard,
1939–   joint author. II. Title.
TH4819.M6R32   643   75–8296
ISBN 0–8129–0570–9
ISBN 0–8129–6265–6 pbk.

*For Jefferson Max, Mark, and Glenn,
and their generation.*

Many have helped us with the preparation of this book. We would like to extend our thanks to each, but especially to Carol Southern, Emanuel Geltman, and Herbert Nagourney of Quadrangle/The New York Times Book Company. Our two favorite builders, Richard Birk and Harold Bush, have offered us their knowledge and experience; Terry J. Mc-Connell of the Hunterdon County National Bank has painstakingly explained banking practices to us; and our friend and attorney, R. J. Durst II of the firm of Herr and Fisher in Flemington, New Jersey, gave willingly of his time and expertise.

Lastly, thanks are due to the many manufacturers of factory-built housing who have shared their thoughts, experiences, and photographs with us.

J.R./B.R.

CONTENTS

PREFACE

Building your own home is a little like painting a self-portrait—the home and its site will reflect your personality, your way of life.

This book has been written for families for whom money is of the essence, for those of us who cannot afford the luxury of an architect. It is a guide to available manufactured homes that don't empty the pocketbook while they meet the needs and tastes of all who seek a reasonably economical living space.

The forms of construction and types of homes described in this book offer lower costs, especially if you do some of the work yourself, and helpings of self-expression which range from meager to generous. Some homes may not be unique in design, while others are. It costs more to express oneself fully than to do so partially. However, the manufacturers and techniques represented here can offer a much wider range of style and taste than local builders can hope to match.

When one approaches a factory-produced product one must, of necessity, sacrifice an element of quality in the interest of economy. Some mass-produced homes will have fewer fine details, yet may be just as inviting, weatherproof, and comfortable as a custom-designed home, created by an architect especially for a specific client.

A word about architects and builders. An architect can design the ideal home for you, but his services are costly. Many architects also have not been following all of the highly fluid fluctuations of labor and materials as closely as they might. In talking with a number of people on the East Coast, we discovered many instances where budgets had been set by clients and accepted by architects, but once bids were received, the budgets proved to be grossly inadequate. In some cases, construction costs were as much as 50% more than the client's ceiling. We can't imagine anything more useless than a set of plans that the owner can't afford to build.

A situation of this sort is not only expensive, it is a great waste of time—months of consultation, drawing, and soliciting bids down the drain. As one would-be home owner told us, "The architect's plans are the most expensive art drawings I've bought. I can't afford to use them. I might as well frame them." And he did.

Local builders, on the other hand, often select a group of standard plans which they can construct. Frequently they build the homes on acreage which they own and sell the house and land as a single package. Alternatively, they might offer a series of model homes for the customer's inspection and build whichever unit the customer selects, at a stipulated price, either on the customer's land or on land owned by the builder. There is value to thinking of land and home as two separate items, for this enables one to budget accordingly. Some people prefer to spend more on land and less on the home, while others reverse this ratio.

Making alterations to fit a specific lifestyle is difficult and limited in an existing home. Much more latitude is available to those who select plans for a home to be built. Local builders are often affiliated with architects who make the buyer's changes on stock floor plans. Clearly, the possibility for change is greater among homes built from scratch on a site—"stick-built" or "custom" homes—and less among homes coming off an assembly line. Prefabricated housing offers the greatest variation in planning, while mobile and modular homes offer the least flexibility.

Because a house is manufactured either in its entirety or in part does not necessarily mean that the house is cheap. The manufactured housing industry offers a broad price range, with mobile homes on the lower end of the scale and prefabricated homes at the upper end, while modulars are in the middle. However, smaller prefabricated homes may cost less than deluxe mobile homes. In dollars and cents, manufactured housing can be bought for anywhere from $10,000 to more than $100,000 but the vast majority of manufactured homes fall within the $10,000 to $50,000 range.

Building a home—be it with an architect, a local builder, or a manufacturer—is much like going to an automobile showroom to buy a new car. As you look at the price stickers you may be amazed at the number of "extras" listed for each car on the floor. The same car, with slightly different options, can cost hundreds of dollars more than its neighbor with fewer or none of these features.

One home may be equipped with plastic plumbing lines with copper as an option; another might have a larger refrigerator or a poorer-grade stove. One model may have single-pane windows or insulated glass windows; on another, storm doors may be standard. The wise shopper will try to balance these factors with the cost-per-square foot to determine which manufacturer and which model offers the best value per dollar while satisfying the buyer's needs.

As you read this book, bear in mind other factors that contribute to the total cost of building a home, such as the land, local costs for services (digging a well or hooking into an existing water supply; constructing a sep-

tic system or hooking into a sewerage system; electricity tie-in; excavation; foundation; etc.), and whatever legal services are needed for the purchase of the home and, when applicable, land.

One advantage to virtually all of the types of housing in this book is that the costs for the structure itself are set. Once the manufacturer of your choice indicates the price, you know exactly where you stand. This is not always the case with local builders of stick-built homes, for more often than not the home owner ends up paying more than he anticipated. And it has happened that a local builder, unbeknown to the customer, has substituted various items. We do not mean to imply that local builders are unethical, or that all manufacturers of housing are ethical, but it seems to us that you stand a good chance of getting precisely what you pay for with a manufactured house.

Calculating the cost of the unit alone is probably the easiest step. Some manufacturers operate through a network of local representatives, and these men and women offer firm prices for the units they handle as well as estimates of what local services may cost. Bear in mind that these representatives may, perhaps unknowingly, quote low prices for local services in an attempt to encourage a sale, assuming they do none of the constructing.

The prices and specifications listed in this book prevailed at the time the book was written. Remember that as time and "stagflation" march on inexorably, labor and materials rise in cost. (Materials, actually, have been seesawing, rising as a result of inflation, going down as the number of housing starts declines. One manufacturer said he was quoting prices for a 10-day period from the date of his quotation because of the fluid nature of the lumber industry.)

In writing this book we repeatedly contacted more than 700 manufacturers throughout the United States. More than 100 responded, and these are the manufacturers represented here.

During the course of our research we saw the extent to which the industry itself is in flux. A number of firms initially contacted have gone under, and given the present economic prognosis, we would expect that others may follow suit.

It is impossible to write about each and every unit being manufactured. We've tried to focus on the norms and to stress the unusual.

Here are a few suggestions for using this book. First, try to locate the area where you want to live (the checklist following the introduction will be useful). Then go through this book selecting those manufacturers (listed at the end of each chapter) whose homes are in harmony with your taste, budget, and site. Write to the manufacturers for their literature, price lists, specifications lists, and names of local representatives.

Take this book and the manufacturers' information to the local building inspector if he must approve your home. If he will not approve the specific home you have in mind, find out, using this book, which type of home he will approve.

Don't be put off by all the steps and details. Take the whole process slowly, with measured tread.

We'd like very much to know how you fare. If you can, write to us in care of the publisher, Quadrangle/The New York Times Book Company, 10 East 53rd Street, New York, New York 10022.

Good luck.

JUDITH AND BERNARD RABB
Kingwood Township, New Jersey

GOOD SHELTER

*A Guide to Mobile, Modular, and
Prefabricated Houses, Including Domes*

INTRODUCTION

Owning a home—"a building for human habitation," as the *Oxford English Dictionary* defines it—is the great American dream. Our present concept of a home goes further than the definition, for we in America tend to seek more than a building that will keep us dry and warm. We demand more than a large enclosed room in which to eat, sleep, and enjoy private recreations. We insist upon separate spaces for specific purposes—a kitchen for the preparation of food, a dining room for guests, a living room for entertaining ourselves and friends, bedrooms and bathrooms for privacy. And many also seek dens, family rooms, playrooms, studies, libraries, attics, and basements.

We have taken the basic word "house" and expanded its meaning to encompass not only shelter, but also the kind of life each of us hopes to lead. A "house" can be an old gingerbread Victorian with nooks and crannies, a farmhouse on an isolated dirt road, a suburban modular ranch on a quarter-acre lot, a mobile home in a park or on its own parcel of land, or a prefabricated modern home located on a large parcel of land or a small building lot.

No one would disagree that the more elaborate the taste requirements, the more expensive the home. In the past, individual homes, custom built ("stick-built") or manufactured, tended to get larger and more luxurious with each passing year. Recession and inflation have cut deeply into the housing industry: materials fluctuate in cost; labor costs are rising; the cost of transporting the units is increasing; the cost of mortgage money is very expensive. As a result, the number of housing starts in the nation has been decreasing at an alarming rate, causing widespread unemployment and virtually halting the sale of new homes. That people are uncertain about the economic future hurts the housing industry, for people tend to stay put, in some cases building additions to their homes rather than looking for new, larger homes.

As a result of mounting costs and the overall economic malaise, we anticipate that more and more manufacturers will scale their products down, providing smaller units with fewer frills at lower costs. Housing as an industry may well change its focus from a provider of comfort to a provider of basic shelter. And in the process, the industry will also conserve natural resources.

Housing may well be a replay of the woes of the automotive industry, which as a whole did not respond quickly to the public's interest in smaller cars of lower sticker price and higher mileage per gallon. Just as Detroit's automobile manufacturers have been offering rebates and hinting at better deals, we suspect that housing manufacturers also will be likely to make deals to move their inventories.

What should a home be like? It should be warm in winter and comfortable in summer. It should provide the kinds of space needed by those living within. Rooms should be arranged to maximize individual privacy. The home should be sited on its land in such a way as to provide the fullest enjoyment of the natural environment, and the exterior design of the home should harmonize with the land.

The Site and Placement

The physical characteristics of the land will, to a degree, define the kind of home which would be best. Ranch houses, which are low and long, can be set attractively on flat, empty land. Bi-levels require sloping terrain to be economical and attractive; a two-story home should have the benefit of trees, as should a split-level.

Houses on wooded lots have the advantage of natural shade and privacy and the disadvantage of less than maximum natural light and heat from the sun. Heavily shaded homes are cooler in summer, paint on the exterior does not tend to blister, and the possibility of warpage of wooden siding is reduced.

The converse is true for homes built on open land. Owners of open land hopefully will see fit to plant trees near their homes, for shade, privacy, and esthetics.

When we speak of trees for shade we are referring to trees with leaves as opposed to needle evergreens which maintain their color throughout the year but offer little in the way of shade. Evergreens, however, are good screens when planted close together.

Whatever you plant—bushes, hedges, or trees—these additions invariably enhance the value of your property. Landscaping is a very good investment, especially if you plant small trees and shrubs that will grow to substantial size by the time you plan to move elsewhere. Plan your planting carefully, and be sure not to plant shrubs or trees that will grow to large size too close to the house, because they can create maintenance problems.

The procedure for siting your home on the land is direct and logical. Walk the land and see where, optionally, you would like the home to be, bearing in mind grades for water runoffs and driveways. Remember that the less steep the grade of your driveway, the easier it will be to get your car in and out in the event of a heavy snow. The land near the foundation wall should slope away from your

(DECK HOUSE)

home so that water from rain or melting snow does not accumulate at the foundation and seep into the foundation and basement. With your floor plans in hand, visit the site and decide where you want morning and afternoon sun and heat, and that will help you to orient your house.

Mark the land with stakes to indicate the lay of the house. One stake at each angle of the house should do the trick.

Warm in Winter, Cool in Summer, and Dry in Wet Weather

A physically warm interior is provided by the builder in two ways: he insulates the structure with materials designed to keep heat inside the home and he provides a system for heating the space (forced hot air, electric, or a hot water radiation system). The objective is to use the heating system as efficiently as possible to keep fuel bills at a minimum. Psychological warmth is also important, and the home should have comfortable and inviting interiors.

The insulation in the walls also helps to keep the home cool in hot weather. Ample windows, trees, awnings, roof overhangs, and even trellises keep temperatures down inside the home.

Your home should also be dry. The house should be so well built and properly sited that water will not accumulate in your basement, nothing will mildew, and your roof will not leak.

Good Interior Spaces

Rooms should be of a size adequate for their purposes. Your own life-style is the criterion. Ask yourself what each room will be used for, how many people will use it at one time, and the amount of furniture needed for these purposes. As you study floor plans, check especially for the location of air duct outlets or heating units, for you will not be able to use those areas for furniture placement.

A good hint in judging space and space capability is to measure all your furniture

(AMERICAN BARN)

and, using graph paper, make cutouts of the furniture to scale. Then, using the same scale and the same graph paper, make an outline of the room and place the cutout furniture on the grid (no furniture over low air outlets or in front of baseboard or radiator units). This will give a very accurate picture of what will fit and how much room will be left for moving around. Don't forget to indicate all closet units. Closets with sliding doors are no problem, but closet doors that open out will prevent placing furniture immediately next to the hinges or in areas where the door knob might dent the furniture. Bi-fold doors are becoming increasingly popular because of their ease of use and because, when open, one can see the entire contents of the closet.

Exterior Design

The manufactured housing industry offers a wide range of exterior design, which is especially useful to those of you who might not wish to build a California mission-style home with a tile roof in Maine or a Southern plantation-style home in Idaho.

Not only does architecture differ across the country, but materials change too. Brick is especially popular in the South, as protection against dampness and termites. In New England the reverse is true. Adobe and stucco are used in some areas but are not found elsewhere.

Floor Plans

The floor plan—the size of each room and its relationship to the other rooms of the home—is entirely dependent on the needs of the buyer. Floor plans tend to be rather standard for manufactured and stick-built housing, but quite a bit of change is possible.

We suggest that you work from strength when you consider floor plans. Design a floor plan that is optimal for your needs. To help you do this, we have included a number of questions for your consideration in the checklist following this chapter. Then

think about your traffic patterns—who carries what where and how often, which parts of the house will get the most usage and why.

After you have created your "dream floor plan," try to find a plan that approximates it and is available at a price you can afford.

Machinery

A house is a conglomeration of contraptions with moving parts—refrigerator, stove, water pump, water heater, furnace, dish washer, clothes washer, clothes dryer, etc. A house is a giant electrical outlet to accommodate all of the trappings of twentieth-century living. Which of these things do you need? Do you need the "deluxe" models —frost-free refrigerators, refrigerators that dispense club soda while whistling *Happy Days Are Here Again,* self-cleaning ovens, quick-recovery water heaters, etc. and can you afford what you need? Can you afford what you want?

Many housing manufacturers will tell you just what kind of equipment and appliances are supplied with the units they sell, and it is your responsibility to check out the items yourself in terms of overall quality, frequency of repair record, and value. We therefore suggest that you read through the publications of consumer testing groups, such as *Consumer Reports,* for their comments, which are especially useful when you come across an unfamiliar brand name.

Maintenance and Upkeep

Many people prefer homes that require a minimum of maintenance, especially for the exterior. Plan for this convenience and economy in advance by carefully checking the siding materials each manufacturer uses. Here, too, personal taste comes into play, for you may not especially care for aluminum siding, which is common within the housing industry and easy to maintain. Other forms of siding, such as cedar shakes and shingles, require some maintenance and are initially more expensive than aluminum.

Cedar in its natural form changes color as it weathers. After about fifteen years you might use a coat of wood refresher to keep the wood in good condition, and from time to time, a shake or shingle may fall from the roof or exterior wall and need replacing, but that is just about all the maintenance cedar shakes and shingles require.

Clapboard siding, an attractive alternative, requires periodic painting. One can readily buy aluminum and hardboard siding which simulate clapboard. Note the word "simulate."

Manufactured Housing—The Three Forms

The National Association of Building Manufacturers (NABM) defines the three forms of manufactured housing as follows:

Mobile homes: "Factory-assembled non-permanent structures usually 8' to 14' in width and 32' or more in length built on a chassis for hauling to a site where it need not comply with the prevailing building code. Usually financed as chattel property, taxed as a vehicle or personal property."

Modular homes: "A permanent structure consisting of one or more modules assembled in a factory in accordance with a building code, and qualified to be financed and taxed as real property when placed on a permanent foundation."

Prefabricated homes: "Factory-assembled components to be shipped to a site for assembly to form a building or house structure."

Mobile Homes

Despite its name, the mobile home is not designed to be placed on its site on a Monday and moved on Wednesday. The name is used because these homes can be transported relatively easily, and they are built for travel, but the amount of travel to which they should be exposed is limited.

The definition cited above by the NABM, particularly the label "non-permanent," could well arouse the members of the Mobile Homes Manufacturers Association. (The NABM represents modular and prefabricated housing manufacturers.) Mobile home manufacturers define their product as

A double-wide mobile home (LAKEWOOD INDUSTRIES)

follows: "A mobile home is a transportable structure, which exceeds 8 body feet in width or 32 body feet in length, built on a chassis and designed to be used as a dwelling with or without a permanent foundation when connected to the required utilities." The questions of permanence, financing, and building codes are discussed elsewhere in this book.

Modular Homes

Modular homes are transported but once, from the factory to the actual site, where they are placed on foundations. They are permanent residences. Modular homes as they are manufactured in the United States today are usually two separate sections, or modules, which are attached when both are placed on the foundation. Almost all manufacturers of modular homes in the United States provide two units which when attached form a rectangle. (There are several exceptions, including one manufacturer who offers modular A-frames.) There is no reason, in theory, why modular homes cannot be constructed of more than two units, or within other geometric forms, but so far the industry has not exactly been a trail-blazer in creating exciting designs using new concepts.

Modular homes, though they serve a very useful function in the detached dwellings market, best illustrate their enormous versatility in large developments of apartment houses, town houses, etc.

Prefabricated Housing

This, the most expensive of the three forms, is also known as "component" housing, for pre-cut or pre-assembled sections are delivered to the site and then each of the parts or sections is placed into position by a skilled crew or sometimes by the buyer himself.

Because prefabricated housing comes in parts of a standard size, it can readily lend itself to "custom" design. In our opinion, prefabricated homes can better satisfy individual taste than so-called stick-built and custom homes built by local contractors. Of the three forms of housing in this book, prefabricated housing has the greatest variety of design and use of space. Many are superb homes which have won architectural design awards.

Domes

Domes are a form of prefabricated building. The exterior of the dome is often delivered by truck in sections, and the pre-cut, pre-assembled triangular panels are then attached on the site. The dome allows the greatest interior flexibility, for it is entirely self-supported and does not depend on interior posts or walls for support. One can have rooms wherever and of whatever size one wishes. But little variation can be achieved on the exterior unless one creates one's own dome shape from one's own geometrical calculations.

On a cost per square-foot basis, domes are probably the cheapest of the prefabricated homes.

Why Manufactured Housing?

Three good reasons—money, time, and variety. Manufactured housing generally costs less than comparable stick-built homes. Manufactured housing can be ready for occupancy in a much shorter time than stick-built homes. And, as you might guess, with hundreds of manufacturers active in the country, the customer has greater variety to choose from. The more you have to spend, the greater the possibility of finding your dream house.

The speed with which manufactured homes can be erected accounts in part for the lower costs. Virtually all manufactured homes are constructed for the most part on an assembly line, where skilled and unskilled workers using highly sophisticated equip-

A bi-level modular home

A split-level prefabricated home (NATIONAL HOMES)

ment can produce more with a high degree of efficiency and accuracy than an individual builder could hope to do.

Manufactured housing is made the year round in enclosed factories. Stick-built homes—especially in those parts of the country with severe winters—are more dependent upon weather conditions; much construction comes to a halt in dead of winter, and it may be further delayed by the spring rains. Weather conditions can affect manufactured housing too, being critical for foundation work, and weather conditions can delay the transportation of the units.

Factory assembly lines can lower the per-unit cost to the consumer by producing each unit faster, using unskilled labor, and purchasing materials in quantity for greater economy. They also produce a product which, in theory, should have a lower margin of error. The great disadvantage of mass production is its uniformity. Because of the high expense of establishing an assembly line and tooling, the mass-produced

home is designed to appeal to the single largest group of potential buyers and may offer little in the way of individuality. This is especially true of modular and mobile home manufacturers and less true of prefabricated home manufacturers.

Another cost saving in manufactured housing is the hidden cost of vandalism. The local contractor may find this a serious problem at a building site, but an enclosed factory could have better security precautions. The contractor undoubtedly passes along the cost of theft to the consumer.

Commenting on the potential economy of manufactured housing as contrasted with stick-built homes, Richard L. Bullock, Executive Vice President of the National Association of Building Manufacturers, wrote:

> One of the biggest factors contributing to the growth of industrialized building is the dwindling supply of trained craftsmen in the construction trades. As the nation has grown, apprentice

Fully assembled walls and framing in the factory (NEW ENGLAND HOMES)

training rates have declined, creating a major shortage of skilled workmen which now appears to be affecting every construction trade in every United States market. This, of course, makes it impossible to meet the nation's housing needs using traditional techniques.

The tradesmen shortage has in turn created another problem, an upward spiral in labor costs far greater than that of other types of workers. This wage spiral has played a major part in accelerating construction costs to all-time highs.*

Aside from the enormous increases in labor costs, Bullock's statement leads to an obvious conclusion: supply cannot meet demand for inexpensive housing. One solution, as valid today as it was during the Industrial Revolution, is mass production. Manufactured housing, a relative newcomer on the scene, has already placed more than 4 million Americans in modular or prefabricated homes and an estimated 6 million in mobile homes.

The checklist and discussion that follow cover major decisions you will make and the nitty-gritty details which, when put together, will hopefully add up to a home in an area that you will enjoy fully. Please give the checklist plenty of thought. There are no shortcuts in building a home.

You may find that some questions do not apply to you. If so, just go on to the next item. Don't hesitate to make copies of any of the checklists in this book for each parcel of land you are considering buying and for each manufactured home you are thinking about. The checklists are also valid for stick-built homes available from local builders and for architect-designed homes as well.

Before you set foot into a real estate broker's office, know what you are looking for and what you can afford: a building lot

* Richard L. Bullock. "Industrialized Building: Where It's At . . . Where It's Going," *1972 Builders Guide to Manufactured Homes,* published by the National Association of Building Manufacturers, Washington, D.C.

or large acreage; a rural, suburban, or urban area; a year-round home or vacation residence. Set a rough budget for yourself for land and home—what percentage of that figure is for the land, and what percentage is for the home?

Think big.

Selecting a Community

Must the land be near a metropolitan area? If so, how close (in miles or minutes)? _____

Do you prefer a suburban setting? Small town? Semirural setting? Rural setting?

Are real estate taxes high, moderate, or low?

Is the total cost of your house and land commensurate with prices in the immediate area? (If your home is substantially more expensive than your neighbors' homes you may not recover your costs when selling.)

Will friends and social activities be drawn from the community or elsewhere?

How close should the home be to employment (in miles or minutes)? _____

How will you get to work (car or public transportation or both)? Are car pools available?

How close is the land to daily shopping (in miles or minutes)? _____ How will you get there?

How many cars will your family need?

Are the public schools good? If not, are private schools located nearby and how will your children get there (your car or school bus)? Are facilities available nearby for special education? Higher education? Adult education?

Is there a good supply of doctors? Is a hospital convenient? Is there local ambulance service or a rescue squad?

Is local police protection provided?

Is local fire protection provided?

Is a local library available and convenient?

Are cultural facilities available?

Are religious facilities available?

Are entertainment facilities available?

What recreational facilities are available (itemize)? _____

_____

Is a public water supply available? (If not, you will have to dig your own well.)

Is public sewerage available? (If not, you will have to install your own septic system.)

Are local roads good? Will your land be convenient to state and interstate highways?

The Real Estate Broker

Your responses to the checklist will roughly define the type of community you seek and its location. Enter the real estate broker. He or she will show you land for sale. As you deal with brokers, bear in mind that they have but one function: to make a sale from which they will receive a commission. Their fees are paid only upon the conclusion of the sale; the usual practice is that the seller pays the broker's commission; however, the buyer is actually paying the commission because the purchase price of the land includes the commission.

The broker's fee is a percentage of the purchase price. Obviously, the broker does not mind having the land sell for more, while the buyer is hoping to buy it for less. When you see property you want, make an offer that would be attractive to you. Even though the broker may say that your offer

is unacceptable to the seller, he is obligated to present your offer to the seller, who has the right to tell the buyer to go soak his head.

No matter how dignified the process of buying land may appear, it is nothing more than a matter of haggling and bargaining, even when the broker says the price is firm.

Brokers do strange things. When we were looking for a house to buy in 1968, we calculated that we wanted to spend a maximum of $25,000. We told a broker our budget, and the first house he showed us was about $17,000 more than we had in mind. It was lovely. We told the broker to give the seller our bid of $25,000. The broker laughed (so did the seller), and we went off to the next property. It took the broker about three months to realize that we were not fooling. Eventually we found what we were looking for at our price. Brokers are convinced that buyers can always find an additional $6,000 or $10,000 somewhere. Sometimes this money can be found, but usually buyers do not want to use every cent of income to support a house.

You will find that some brokers make an effort to know a great deal about the properties they show, while others are little more than glorified chauffeurs.

Brokers, by the way, have a curious language. They use words—in conversation and newspaper advertising—we all understand, and charming clichés, but their meanings are sometimes alien to buyers. Here are a few of these phrases, with definitions of what they really mean.

"Peaceful setting"—at least 100 yards from an airport.

"Charming country village"—old and expensive.

"Quaint country village"—old and run-down.

"The hounds are off"—the broker's implication is that the land is in fox-hunting country, but the real meaning is that the land is next to a kennel.

"Zoned industrial"—the last time the broker looked.

"Must sell"—present owner has discovered that the land is in the flood plain; the property is shown only in July and August.

"Alpine-like"—be prepared to be snowed-in all winter.

"View of the river"—from the upper right-hand corner of the bathroom window.

"Over 1 acre"—but a lot less than 2 acres.

Chances are very good that you'll get the hang of brokerese after the first hour or so.

Once you find suitable land, ask around about it: Does it flood? Is a nuclear plant scheduled to be built a hundred yards from the boundaries? Is the road in front of the property used by trailer trucks which make deliveries at 4 A.M.?

The Site

Take a close look at the land itself, beginning with its physical characteristics.

Is the land flat or does it slope? If it slopes, can a home be constructed in an economical manner, or are special engineering and construction needed?

Where will water drain off?

How much grading (changing the existing terrain) will be necessary once the home is built?

Do subsoil conditions permit economical excavating? What is the depth to bedrock?

What is the approximate depth to water if you have to dig your own well?

If the land has trees, will any of them have to be removed during construction?

How can you use the remaining trees to best advantage? How can you keep as many trees as possible?

Is there surface water (brook, pond, swamp) on the land? If so, how far, in feet, between water and home? _____ Water and drilled well? _____ Water and septic system? _____ Will your driveway cross the surface water and require a bridge?

Does the land offer any special scenic views that you wish to take advantage of? If so, which rooms of your home should have

"Unimproved" land

the scenic exposure? Are there any unscenic views to avoid?

Where will the driveway be located? How long, in feet, will the driveway be? _____ Will the driveway be steeply graded?

Have you planned for adequate parking space? Is there adequate turning space for cars?

Services

Utilities are a major budgetary concern. Here are some things to consider.

Does the municipality offer a public water system, or will you have to dig your own well?

Does the municipality offer public sewerage, or will you have to build your own septic system? If you provide your own septic system, precisely what kind and size of system is required by local law? Have a soil percolation test and soil log taken if you are installing a septic system.

Does the municipality provide garbage collection?

Does the electric company offer a choice of higher or lower amperage service?

Does the telephone company offer a variety of lines—private, semi-private, party? How bad (or good) is local telephone service?

As you look at the land, think site development. Draw a map of the property, locate the house, driveway, all other buildings regardless of when you can afford to build them, and all possible outdoor uses. For each of the outdoor uses given below, you should evaluate the inherent requirements of size, topography, sun and wind, views, and subsoil conditions and then consider suitability, function, and relation to the house and road.

Here is a list of uses for land: lawns, flower and/or vegetable garden, barn, garage or carport, patio, play area for children, swimming pool, tennis court, basketball court, other game areas, clothes line, storage sheds, and garbage storage.

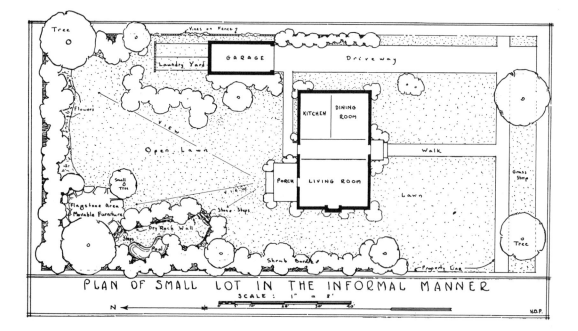

A site plan

Zoning

Generally speaking, the more developed a municipality, the more clearly defined its zoning and building codes. Zoning is a protective measure, protecting, for example, the homeowner in a residential zone from the incursion of a nonresidential use next door. This is fine, in theory, and it should work, but all too often a local municipality may grant a zoning variance for one reason or another and this allows for nonresidential use in a residential zone. Of course, those living in the area affected by the variance can and do wage bitter fights, and they often win. Clearly, municipalities with zoning codes offer greater protection from unwanted incursions than those without any zoning regulations, where anything can happen and the landowner may have no recourse.

Zoning decisions are, however, subject to political pressures from the citizens of a community, from the largest industry in town, or from a builder who intends constructing a massive housing development. So, like just about every other governmental action, zoning can be a mixed bag of blessings and catastrophes.

Before you sign anything, check the zoning ordinances carefully and find out where the land you would like to buy is located. The ordinance will include a map showing each of the zones as well as a description of what is and what is not allowed in each zone. It should be available from the municipal offices. Here are some specifics to resolve:

What uses are permitted on the land?

What is the minimum lot size for a single-family home? Does your property conform?

What is the minimum frontage (in feet) required?

What is the minimum distance (setback) allowed between the house and the land boundaries (courses)? Does this requirement prevent you from siting your home precisely where you wish?

What is the minimum house size (usually expressed in square feet) allowed in the zone? Does your home conform?

Does the municipality place any design restrictions on the house you plan to build? Does the municipality have to approve the design of your house? Does the municipality require you to submit the design of your house to an architectural review committee of some sort?

What are the zones adjacent to your land?

How far from these zones will your land be?

What uses are permitted in these adjacent zones?

What plans exist for the future development in the area which might affect you? Should you rethink your intention to buy land in this location?

Building Codes

The next step is to check the building codes of the municipality. This is especially critical, for some building codes may not permit the type of manufactured home you plan to construct. Others may require that the structure, though assembled elsewhere, conform to the prevailing local code.

Once you know whether the type of home you intend to buy—mobile, modular, or prefabricated—is permitted, you can begin comparing the manufacturer's specifications against those of the codes. Your real estate broker or lawyer should have copies of these codes, or you can buy them from the clerk or building inspector. In principle, these codes are written for the protection of the person building a new home, and they should be approached as a benefit despite the petty annoyances which they might create.

The same could be said of the building inspector. He is a public servant charged with enforcing the building code which has been created as a safeguard. If he is concerned with shoddy construction, you should be even more concerned, because you'll be living in the house. The building inspector is,

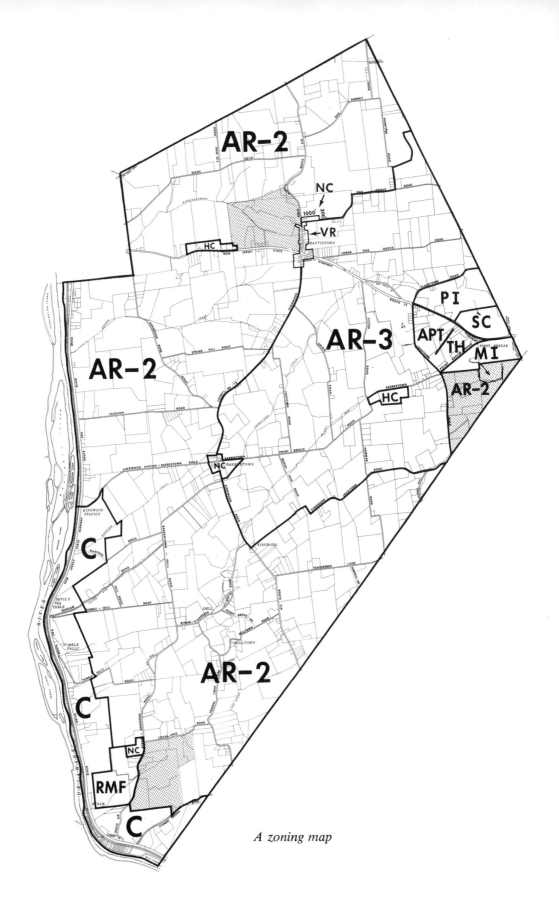

A zoning map

in a sense, a professional consultant who is paid by the municipality.

The inspector is required to check every facet of the construction of your home and the installation of services. This is no problem for prefabricated home manufacturers whose products are assembled on the site in full view of the inspector. But it is of major concern for mobile and modular manufacturers, who provide a complete dwelling that arrives from the factory entirely assembled. How can the building inspector fulfill his function? Should he rip out a few walls or some of the floors to check the structure? Unless he visits the factory and watches the construction of the specific unit intended for his municipality, he cannot do his job properly on a mobile or modular home.

Furthermore, building inspectors run the daily gamut of local stick-built contractors trying to chisel here and skimp there, and you can imagine the jaundiced eye they will level at a specifications list from a manufacturer who may be hundreds of miles away and in a different state.

As a result of the problem facing mobile and modular manufacturers, and to safeguard the people who will live in these homes, many states have instituted statewide building codes for these forms of housing. Your lawyer should have copies of these codes, and it would be wise for you to check the codes against the specifications lists of those manufacturers in whose products you have interest. Further, the manufacturer might not indicate, upon receipt of your order, that his unit is not acceptable in the area you have chosen. However, if you buy through a local dealer you can be reasonably sure that the units he sells are acceptable in the state.

If your state has a modular and mobile home building code, and the municipality where you hope to live subscribes to this code, you should have no problems, assuming that the product you buy is acceptable under the provisos of that code. Many states will send their own inspectors, unannounced, to plants throughout the country to inspect and certify those units which are intended for sale in those states.

If no building codes exist where you plan to settle, you might still like the assurance of some level of quality control, for materials and construction techniques. Many units are approved by Federal agencies like FHA and VA. If you are applying to the VA, FHA, or Farmers Home Administration to guarantee a loan, you must purchase a home whose construction has been approved by the agency. Also, most manufacturers will indicate in their brochures those agencies that have approved various models.

Does the municipality (whichever branch of government having jurisdiction over building) allow mobile homes? Modular homes? Prefabricated homes, including domes?

Does the municipality have a building code? Does the home you plan to build meet or better the requirements of the building code?

Does the municipality have a plumbing code? Does your home meet or better it? Heating code? Electrical code?

Buying a Manufactured House

Most manufactured housing is sold by a representative or agent of the manufacturer; in some cases the buyer deals directly with the manufacturer. An important point to check is the reputation for reliability of the manufacturer and his representative. One way of getting some answers is to ask for a list of people in the area who live in homes purchased from the manufacturer and representative. Visit a few of them, if you can, and put these questions to them:

How is the home holding up?

Any major problems requiring repair? Did the dealer/representative or manufacturer correct any faults quickly or did he provide adequate compensation?

How long did it take to resolve the difficulties?

Are they satisfied with the services provided by the dealer and manufacturer?

Was the home ready for occupancy when promised?

Do they have any recommendations of lawyers, contractors, etc.?

Have they any hints for you?

Lawyers, Lawyers, Lawyers

Assuming the land you wish to buy falls within the correct zone and the seller accepts your verbal offer, you will place a deposit, sometimes called "earnest money," of about $100 to $500. Brokers will often prepare a binder for signature by buyer and seller. Your attorney should review it. The next step is the contract, usually drawn by the seller's attorney, which indicates that the seller will sell a designated parcel of land to the buyer on a given date. A payment of 10% of the sale price is required when the buyer signs the contract.

The contract will also state any contingencies which, if not met by either party, will void the sale. For example, the buyer should make the sale contingent upon receiving a mortgage; contingent upon receiving a satisfactory percolation test if the local government requires it; contingent upon the building inspector's approval of the specific type of housing the buyer wishes to erect; contingent upon a survey, which shows exactly how much land is involved in the sale; contingent upon a free-and-clear title, which means that the seller has the right to sell the property; and contingent upon any strange easements which the deed of sale may include. Other contingencies may be added by your lawyer, who hopefully will have a sharp knowledge of local real estate practices.

You can also expect the seller to have at least one contingency—that you guarantee, within a specified period of time, that you have received whatever mortgage commitments from a lending institution you need to buy the land. If you are paying cash, you have no problems.

In our opinion, it is imperative for the buyer to have his own lawyer. In some cases the seller might magnanimously offer to save the legal fees for you if you allow his attorney to represent both buyer and seller. It sounds tempting, but if you accept the gesture you will always wonder, especially if you encounter any problems, just whose side the attorney was on.

A word of caution about the deposit and earnest money. Issue this deposit in the name of the real estate broker's escrow account and under no circumstances should you give a deposit directly to the seller, either in cash or check. If you have any problems later on, before the sale, this money might be difficult, if not impossible, to recover. The seller should see the color of your money only on the day of the sale, or "closing."

Your lawyer should enter the picture before the contract of sale is drawn. He will do whatever negotiating is necessary with the seller or the seller's attorney, though the broker may also attempt to represent you with the seller.

A land survey is an invaluable document, and you should have one even if you have to pay for it yourself. Surveys are generally easy to come by on land recently subdivided, and the seller should make the survey available to the buyer at no cost. Surveys can be problematical and expensive where large tracts of land are involved.

The survey will tell you exactly how much land is in the parcel, all of the courses, and the names of all who hold land which abuts the property. It also identifies each course by longitude and latitude, and this description should appear on the deed of sale. The old style of land description— "about 20 feet to the old black walnut tree" or "15 feet along the old stone wall"— though quaint, is too unscientific in the event of a later dispute.

We remember buying a property in New Jersey from a sharp Massachusetts Yankee. The broker's listing showed 5 acres; the seller said that almost 10 acres were involved. The survey showed the property to be 4.9 acres. "Show me" should be the buyer's motto, and a survey does just that.

The first day we met the Massachusetts Yankee, we agreed on a price, following

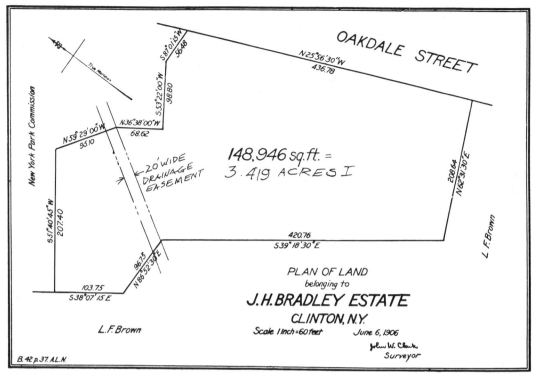

A survey with easement and right-of-way shown

which the seller asked us to "lend" him $35 for gas to get back to Massachusetts. How he settled on $35, at 1968 gas prices, from New Jersey to Boston, we'll never know. We said no and he tried the same gambit on the broker, threatening to cancel the deal if he didn't get his money. The broker refused, too, and the deal went through (not before the seller told us that $10,000 in cash was stashed away somewhere in the house; not before we had to remove a "cloud" on the property by having a 90-year-old woman in a Massachusetts nursing home sign a document; and not before seeing the sheriff present a summons to the seller just before the closing—but that's another story).

But getting back to the survey, accept no substitute for a survey prepared by a licensed surveyor. Do not accept a sketch, either by the broker or the seller, drawn from memory or from a tax map. Your lawyer can probably recommend someone if you have to arrange for the survey yourself.

If the survey is acceptable to you, the buyer, which means that the seller did not misrepresent the amount of land for sale, you can go to the next step—a title search. The title search proves that the seller can sell the property. It will be done by a title searcher who traces the ownership of the land back as much as 100 years or more. It is a lesson in local history.

The search will also uncover any easements granted by the seller or previous sellers, which might affect your building plans, such as a right-of-way to the telephone company which, if ever enforced, would place a telephone pole in the middle of your living room. Easements are often granted to telephone, electric, and gas companies, and you should be sure that the path of the easement is away from your home, and away from any recreational areas (swimming pool, tennis court, etc.) which you may be planning for the future.

You may also come across rights-of-way which have been granted by a previous owner. A right-of-way is nothing more than the right for someone else to cross your property at a specified place to get to another property, on foot, on horseback, in a car, in a truck. The land is yours. Again, don't plan to do any major building on or near the right-of-way. A right of way, like an easement, may never be used, but then again (if you are feeling paranoid) it might be put into use the Monday after you move into your new home.

Another thing to watch is the restrictive covenant—a restriction of some sort which has been set by a previous owner and which passes down to every successive owner. Let's say, for argument's sake, that a previous owner did not like houses with decks. He could write a restrictive covenant into his deed of sale to the next owner, stating that no home with a deck can be built upon the land.

Assuming the search uncovers unacceptable rights-of-way, easements, or covenants there is a way out. You can offer to buy back these rights from whoever owns them, but this can be very expensive, even though the original rights were purchased for very small sums.

If the title search raises no obstacles; advance to the deed.

Perhaps the most important thing to remember is to ask your lawyer about anything that is of concern and to read everything which requires your signature and money. Read the contract and deed carefully, make sure all of the points you wanted included are in the documents, and that the land description is accurate. We remember once going through a deed of sale. Our lawyer swore that each and every line was checked under a magnifying glass. Being ornery, we read the deed and found that somewhere along the line one of the courses had been omitted and a second had been duplicated. The moral: A layman's eye, unaccustomed to legal language, can be more accurate than an attorney's. Read everything.

Finally comes the closing, a lengthy and turgid *pas de deux* between attorneys during which each tries to show his client that his fee is deserved. The closing can be at an attorney's office or at a bank. The buyers and sellers are there, supplemented by an officer of the bank and the broker, who quietly sits in a corner twiddling his thumbs until the instant when money passes between the buyer and the seller. The buyers and sellers, their attorneys, and the banker all shake hands and smile. The broker extends his hand, palm up, for his fee. The large amounts of money going back and forth across the table will stagger you, but that is part of the closing rite.

Consider filing for title insurance, which your bank may even insist upon. It is a one-time expenditure that is not too costly, and it will insure you against any claims that might be brought against your deed in the future.

With land in hand, you will need your lawyer's assistance on whatever contracts are to be signed with the manufacturer of your house and whatever contractors or builders are called in for the other steps involved in preparing a home for occupancy. Bear in mind that your attorney has two functions— to make sure that all contracts and documents have been properly drawn and to make sure that his client gets the best possible shake.

Your lawyer will have much to say about your contract for the residence. One of the areas you might explore with your attorney is the question of penalty clauses in the contract with the manufacturer or contractor. The penalty clause is designed to spur the completion of your home on time by penalizing the other side a specified amount for each day of delay.

If the completion date is missed, much difficulty can face the buyer. He and his family may have to find a place (hotel, motel) to live and a place to store possessions (including trucking from the former dwelling to a warehouse and from the warehouse to the new home). Money and inconvenience are involved here.

The penalty clause does have a psychological handicap, however. You can reason that the builder faced with a penalty clause will do his utmost to finish the house, perhaps even rushing work so as to avoid the penalty. On the one hand, you want to move in on a specified date; on the other hand, you may get substandard workmanship from the builder. If a penalty clause is inserted in your contracts, it should involve moderate amounts so that the builder or manufacturer is not forced into a serious loss situation. The builder who watches every penny of profit will deliver on time, regardless of quality. Hopefully, you will find someone who takes pride in his work and who will take the time to do the job properly. If you are lucky enough to find such a builder, you might consider waiving the penalty clause if you feel that the delay might not have been the builder's fault but may have resulted from a particular circumstance outside the builder's control.

If shortly after you have moved in and after the manufacturer and/or local skilled labor have been paid in full, you come across shoddy construction, what do you do? You call the person responsible. If he is conscientious, he will make good. If he is not, or if he thinks the issue is your fault, he will simply avoid you, and you may face a lengthy court suit.

Not long ago, a New Jersey municipality considered adding performance bonds to its building code for individual homes. The builder and/or manufacturer would be required to post a performance bond with the local government which would be refunded when it became clear that all work had been done carefully and professionally. Performance bonds are common throughout the country for work in which local governments are involved. Why should they not be used to provide the same protection for individual home buyers? This is another point to ask your attorney about. Be assured that if you raise this issue with a manufacturer or dealer, he will yell bloody murder. We wish we had a performance bond in our contract for the domes in which we live. We could have saved close to three years of litigation and lawyer's fees, and the repairs would have been made much faster. More about all of this in the dome chapter.

Money

Borrowing money does not cost the same at every lending institution. Some charge more than others—their interest rates may be higher, they may charge "points," or they may chalk on various fees which increases the cost of borrowing money. It always pays to shop around among commercial banks, savings banks, and savings and loan associations, not to mention wealthy relatives and friends.

Lending institutions want more than your interest payments. They want your personal checking account and your savings account (if you have one after you get through building your house). The bank offering a slightly lower interest rate on your mortgage might also offer a lower interest rate on your savings, or might have higher charges for your checking account. You should balance your interest payments to the lending institution against those interest payments and service charges coming from the lender.

The more money you put down as a down payment, the lower your interest rate might be. The longer the term of the mortgage, the more money you will have paid the bank in interest. And the longer the term of the mortgage, the lower the monthly mortgage payment given the same amount of money borrowed.

There are two types of mortgages, ordinary and construction. An ordinary mortgage is granted for a completed structure. Your bank will give you a loan of a percentage of the total price in one lump sum. You turn this money, plus your cash down payment, over to the seller and take possession of the home. A construction mortgage is somewhat different. You and the bank agree upon the amount of the loan. The lending institution will check your contracts with manufacturers and builders for the number of installments to be paid and the amounts per installment. Installments are due upon the satisfactory completion of specified work. You will receive a bill for the work completed, which you take to the bank which then issues you a check in that amount. You usually pay interest only on those amounts dispensed by the bank for completed work.

Aside from checking on fees and points or other hidden charges when you negotiate a mortgage, it is a good idea to look into the area of early payment penalties. Some banks may penalize you if you suddenly are in a position to pay off your mortgage long before the completion of its term. They do this by charging you a specified fee, which you might not like to pay.

Don't be afraid of bankers. Bankers know their communities very well indeed. They know who the good builders and contractors are and may even have lists of those to whom they will not lend money or whom they will not let you use for a variety of reasons. Bankers also know who the good lawyers are and a number of other important pieces of information.

Bankers aren't as conservative as many would believe. When they make a mortgage loan they have but two prime considerations in mind: the ability of the borrower to maintain the monthly payments and the ability of the bank to sell the property in the event the mortgage defaults for at least the amount of money still owed the bank. That's not unreasonable.

In our case, when we built the domes we live in, we had great trepidation as we approached our bank, widely recognized as being the most conservative lending institution in the area. They looked at the plans, considered the costs, considered the amount of floor space within the structure, and concluded that we could make the necessary payments. They granted us our mortgage commitment within four days (they had a special board meeting to study our plans within this time). We concluded that this institution wasn't as conservative as word-of-mouth had it.

The worst that could befall you would be to have a banker say no. Then just go off to the next institution.

Picking a House that Fits

Here is a checklist to help you select a house and floor plan that will do everything you want them to.

What kind of home do you want? One-story? Two-story? One-story over a basement? Two-story over a basement? One-story over a crawl space? Two-story over a crawl space? One-story on a slab? Two-story on a slab? Why? Can you excavate on your land for a basement?

How many bedrooms—1, 2, 3, 4, 5, or more?

After measuring all of your furniture for bedrooms, what size should the master bedroom be? Will this allow for a sitting area? What size should the other bedrooms be? Have you considered ample play and study areas in children's bedrooms?

Where should the bedrooms be? Together in one area? Should parents' bedrooms be separate from children's and guests'?

Which rooms should get the morning sun? Which rooms should be dark in the morning? (In cold climates rooms with a southern exposure will be warm in winter afternoons; rooms facing west will be hot in summer afternoons.)

How much square feet of closet space do you estimate you need for the master bedroom? Other bedrooms?

Will the furniture that you own or intend buying fit comfortably in the rooms of the home you intend buying?

Is a guest closet (near the front door) needed? A linen closet?

How many bathrooms—1, 1½, 2, 2½ or more?

Is the main bathroom near the bedrooms? Should it be? Is a private bath or half-bath adjoining the master bedroom desirable?

Is a full or half-bath near the living room desirable? If your home has two or more levels, do you need one or more bathrooms per level?

Is a study needed? Where should it be? A den? Hobby room? Sewing room? Mud room? How large should these rooms be?

Will the floor plan provide adequate privacy and quiet for all rooms?

Will any special equipment be placed in any of these rooms? Do you require special wiring or plumbing? Can the manufacturer accommodate this need?

What do you do and how much time do you spend in your living room and at which times of day? How large should it be?

What relationship exists between the living room and the main entrance? Is this desirable? Will traffic pass through the living room to reach other parts of the house? Is the living room accessible to the dining room? Kitchen? Is it accessible from a family room? Den? Study? Hobby room? Sewing room? Are these accesses desirable?

Do you want a working fireplace in the living room? Other rooms?

What about special equipment in the living room—master TV and FM antenna, bin for firewood, etc.—and can the manufacturer meet the requirements?

Do you need a family room? Who will use it? When? How? Should it be larger or smaller than the living room? Should it be visible from the kitchen if children use it for play? Should it be accessible from the kitchen? Accessible from the living room? Dining room? Should it receive afternoon sun?

Kitchens—eat-in (large enough to accommodate a table with four chairs), working (appliances and counter space only), or with a snack bar (large enough to accommodate a small table with two chairs)? Does it have adequate counter space and storage space? Is it equipped with all appliances? Does the manufactured home have electrical wiring and plumbing for a dishwasher?

Does the kitchen have access to the dining room? Living room? Family room? Outdoor play areas? Convenient access to where you park your car (especially when a week's groceries are to be carried in)?

Is the work area of the kitchen away from the normal flow of traffic? Should the kitchen have morning or afternoon sun? Is the arrangement of the three basic units—sink, stove, and refrigerator (called the "work triangle")—efficient?

A separate dining room or an area off the living room? How many guests would you normally seat for dinner? Is the area allocated for dining adequate for table and chairs and whatever dining room furniture (such as breakfronts) you plan to have?

Should the kitchen be visible from the dining room?

A utility room for clothes washer and/or dryer? Other equipment (water heater, utility sink, electric junction box, etc.) needed here? Will it also be used for storage? How large should it be? Should it be on the same floor with the bedrooms?

What about a basement—full or half? Do subsoil conditions permit a basement? Will the basement be used for bedrooms? Family room? Guest room? Other living rooms? Hobby or game room? Storage? Should it have direct access to the outside? How will you enter the basement from within the home?

How many cars will you have? Do you need a garage or carport? If a garage, will it also be used for workshop and/or storage space? How big should it be? If you work in the garage, should it be partially heated? Is running water needed? Will any heavy equipment requiring special electrical wiring be used? Should the garage be separate or attached to the home? How convenient is it to the kitchen?

Do you anticipate needing additional storage space, perhaps outside, like storage sheds? How many, how big, and where should they be located?

Are there adequate closets in each room?

Are you planning for a deck, enclosed porch, patio, courtyard, atrium? What will you do in these spaces—eating, relaxing, playing? How large should they be? Should these areas have access to any specific rooms in the house? How will you shade these areas from hot summer sun?

How will you landscape your home for privacy? Privacy from what? The street? Neighbors?

This list is long and complicated, but it is important if you wish to reach a reasonable understanding of exactly what it is you need in the way of a house. It may take months for you to answer all these questions, but your complete answers and realization of how you want to live will make your study of floor plans that much easier.

Here is a list of the steps after you purchase the land, get all of the necessary approvals from the building inspector, and select your manufactured home.

Excavate for foundation and lay the foundation.

Drill a well if no public water supply (make a map of the exact location of the well if the cap is underground to facilitate later servicing).

Excavate for the septic tank and lay the bed if public sewerage is not available (again, make a map of the exact location of the tank for periodic cleaning).

Install all rough plumbing before anything comes from the manufacturer, following the manufacturer's plans.

Complete preliminary grading; clear an area sufficiently large so that trucks bearing mobile or modular units or prefabricated parts have turn-around room.

Set the mobile or modular unit(s) on the foundation; attach unit(s) to foundation and, if more than one, to each other; complete exterior and interior finishing; connect water and sewerage lines; install electric service; move in. In the case of prefabricated homes, begin construction as per the manufacturer's explicit instructions.

Will you be ready for the mortgage, the property taxes, the school taxes, the unexpected repairs and routine maintenance, the homeowner's insurance policy, the rising cost of oil and electricity . . . but that's another book. You probably will be ready for a long rest, for a lot of space, quiet, comfort, and happiness.

MOBILE HOMES

(LAKEWOOD INDUSTRIES)

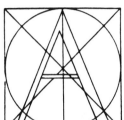mobile home, according to the Mobile Homes Manufacturers Association, is a "transportable structure, longer than 32 feet (and/or) wider than 8 feet, built on a chassis, designed to be used as a dwelling with or without a permanent foundation when connected to the required utilities." It is a self-contained residence which can, but need not, be placed on a permanent foundation and which can be moved from time to time but is not intended to be shunted around the country. The mobile home family intends to settle, for a good while at least, in the exact spot where the structure is first located.

Here are some of the advantages of mobile homes:

1. *Cost.* Mobile homes are the cheapest form of private detached housing available in the United States.

2. *On-site labor.* The cost factor is minimal. No excavating for a foundation is required. The only costs are the installation of services and their connection to the mobile unit. An installation fee for placing the home on its foundation or piers may be charged. Piers or pads are available if the home is located in a mobile home park, but must be purchased if the site is private land.

3. *Mobility.* Though mobile homes are not designed to be moved frequently, they are designed to be moved from time to time, which is an attractive feature for Americans who are themselves highly mobile. It should be stressed that a mobile home cannot be pulled by the family car. Moving a mobile home is a difficult process, requiring expertise by a trailer truck driver in maneuvering on public roads, knowing which roads can be used, how to connect and disconnect service lines, and so forth. In some areas, depending upon the length and width of the unit, state or local police may require special permits before the mobile may use certain roads. In some situations mobile homes may be barred from the roads except for specified times, or local regulations may require that a car with flashers blinking follow the unit.

4. *Instant communities.* Many mobile home parks exist throughout the country. Each park lot has the necessary utilities, and many of these parks offer a variety of recreational and service facilities which can be attractive bonuses. In addition, everyone living in a mobile home park lives in a mobile home, and some people might find this reassuring.

Here's the other side of the coin.

1. *Finance.* Mobile homes are financed much like automobiles; that is, short-term personal loans rather than the mortgages that finance all other forms of housing. The obvious disadvantage is that you have to pay

27

A child's view of a mobile home (MIDLAND COMPANY)

for the unit in a much shorter period of time. And interest rates are often higher than mortgages. This tends to offset some of the lower cost unless you can pay cash. Of course, you save a lot of interest costs by having fewer payments. More about this later.

2. *Lower quality.* Many materials used in mobile homes are generally of a lower quality and building specifications tend to be less stringent than other forms of construction described in this book or conventional stick-built housing. This is one reason that mobile homes tend to depreciate in value, whereas other types of housing tend to appreciate in value as they age.

3. *Size.* Rooms are generally smaller than equivalent rooms in other types of homes, and ceilings tend to be lower.

4. *Floor plans.* A limited range of floor plans is available to the mobile home buyer. This may not be a disadvantage to many. Bear in mind that the ability to change the floor plan of a mobile home is severely limited. You pretty much have to take what is offered or go to another form of housing.

5. *Appearance.* Mobile homes are similar in appearance and all are constructed in pretty much the same manner. There are no unique mobile homes. One attempt to do something about the drabness of these units was aborted before it was even born, and is discussed later.

6. *Safety.* Mobile homes have been blown down by strong winds, even when anchored according to the manufacturer's requirements. As a result of some of their materials, fires in mobile homes spread faster than in conventional homes. The industry has been accused by the Center for Auto Safety of producing homes with built-in fire hazards.

7. *Community acceptance.* This issue has little bearing for those who settle in mobile home parks but is of consequence for those who intend to buy land and site a mobile home on it. Many communities throughout the country object to having mobile homes and have passed local ordinances prohibiting them within their borders. In some cases manufacturers or dealers are challenging the constitutionality of these ordinances. A word to the wise: If the community does not want

a mobile home and can easily get aroused on the issue, it can be very troublesome indeed.

Mobile homes are the cheapest kind of home you can buy. You need fewer dollars to buy a mobile home, but its cost, if extended for the life of the home, may be higher than expected. Still, mobile homes account for an enormous share of all housing constructed in the United States. In 1973, of all homes costing less than $20,000 (a very low figure), 91% were mobiles and they accounted for 48% of all homes of every type and price bracket built that year.

One reason for the low "sticker price" is that mobile homes are generally smaller in area than other forms of housing, with the exception of apartments. The average mobile home is 14′ by 63′ (882 square feet). The 882-square-foot unit is roughly the equivalent of a recently-built three-bedroom apartment with a hallway, working kitchen, living room, and one bathroom. Many manufacturers will quote a unit length which includes a 3′ or 4′ hitch. The manufacturer's quoted length is less important than the total square footage of living area.

Mobile homes average about $8 to $9 per square foot for the entire unit (including furnishings) compared to stick-built homes which start at around $18 per square foot and go up to astronomical levels. Much of the savings differential can be ascribed to several factors: (1) Mobile housing is constructed by unskilled and semiskilled labor (often non-union) in a conveyer-belt operation; (2) manufacturers purchase lower grade materials and in such vast quantities that some of their savings are passed on to the consumer; (3) mobile homes are produced quickly, perhaps as many as ten or more per day in some factories.

Mobile homes are available in a fairly wide range of lengths and in several widths. What follows is data on those units which we were able to research. The so-called single-wides are rectangles between 12′ and 14′ in width and 40′ to 80′ in length. Single-wides start at 12′ × 37′ (usually advertised as 12′ × 40′—we've deducted the hitch), or 444 square feet, at around $4,500 and go up to 14′ × 77′ (advertised as 14′ × 80′), or 1,078 square feet, for about $13,000. The smaller the unit, the higher the cost per square foot, because expensive home equipment and appliances are amortized over a smaller area; the $13,000 unit is loaded with all sorts of luxurious extras.

Double-wides are two single-wides brought to the site separately and joined there. They range in cost from around $6,500 to $25,000 and up. Most double-wides fall within the upper reaches of this dollar range. They are similar to modular homes, which are two equal rectangles placed side by side on a foundation, but double-wide mobiles can be moved and they are not built to the higher specifications of the modulars.

Double-wides range from 40′ to 70′ in length. Standard width is 24′ to 28′. One company, Bendix Home Systems, Inc., offers

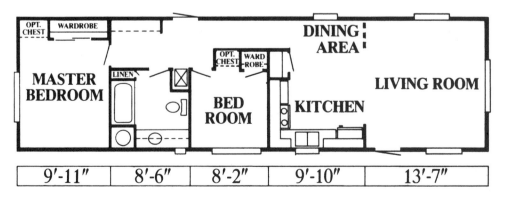

A two-bedroom single-wide mobile home floor plan (BENDIX HOME SYSTEMS, INC.)

A three-bedroom single-wide mobile home floor plan (TOWN & COUNTRY MOBILE HOMES)

a 34′-long double-wide that has about the same floor space as a 64′ × 12′, but its shape is more like that of a conventional home. Two companies, Bendix Home Systems, Inc. and Lakewood, offer 20′-wide homes, and Bonnavilla offers a 26′-wide home.

When most people think of the appearance of a house, they usually envision a rectangular structure made of wood, brick, stone, or cement block (sometimes stuccoed over), sometimes having wooden shutters (which may or may not be fake), and with a pitched roof most often covered with shingles (asphalt or, rarely, cedar). These conventional homes look substantial and solid.

Mobile homes are also rectangular in shape but they lack most of the details that are associated with a "home." Roofs generally have a shallow pitch or are flat, and most are made of aluminum or other metal, as is the siding. Windows and doors are usually small and rarely have even fake shutters (also of aluminum). The proportion of length to width in a single-wide makes it look like a shoe box. Double-wides look more like conventional homes.

But for many, appearance is secondary to function, and the great success of the industry is positive proof that these units are attractively priced and fulfill their purpose.

The fact that the cost of the mobile home

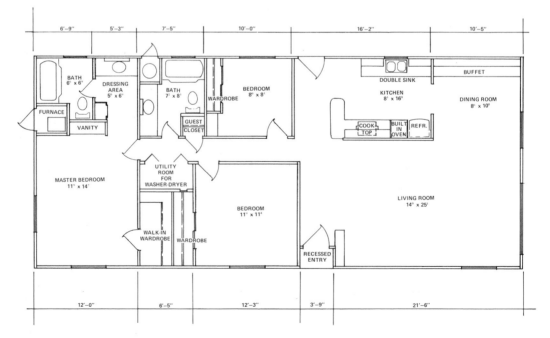

A three-bedroom double-wide mobile home which, unlike most mobile floor plans, is presented with clearly understandable dimensions (DEROSE INDUSTRIES)

also includes flooring (carpets or tile), drapes, furniture, appliances, fixtures, and "decor" makes the already low prices even more appealing (though individual taste and the manufacturer's decor often do not coincide). All you need to move into a mobile home is your clothing, dishes, linens, flatware, and kitchen utensils. The "decor" and details in mobile homes are not what could even generously be termed adventurous or interesting.

Sometimes people buy a mobile home with the intention of adding to the mobile unit at a later date to create a larger residence. This makes good sense, for the mobile unit contains the "core" or basic equipment for any home—plumbing, heating, electrical wiring, and appliances. Additions often consist of new bedrooms and perhaps a larger living room or den. Many people also build porches and patios for their units. When finances permit, some mobile home owners build superstructures above their units when they make additions. A recent newspaper article showed photographs of California mobile homes with superstructures costing as much as $80,000.

A mobile home might be a good idea as a temporary home, but it only makes sense to us if you buy a small, used mobile home, which will later be sold for much less than what you paid for it.

Mobile homes have many potential problems. The Center for Auto Safety recently investigated the industry and published a book with its findings (see the bibliography). It claims that the industry is not well regulated, and some manufacturers feel little or no obligation to correct manufacturer-caused damages. It paints the blackest possible picture of the industry, and you should read it if you are planning to buy a mobile home. Also try to maintain a perspective on the industry, for the book uses a buckshot approach, sometimes unfairly spraying all manufacturers when only a few merit the criticism. We'll be referring liberally to this book as the CAS study.

Where Do You Put a Mobile Home?

About half of all mobile homes in the United States are located on private land; the balance are found in mobile home parks. As with all forms of housing, the land must first be prepared to receive the mobile unit. Concrete runners (pads) or piers must be installed, and utilities must be available prior to the delivery date. The land owner must know exactly where he plans to place the home, and he should also know where his water supply (well or public water system) and disposal system (septic tank or sewage lines) will be. Water and sewage lines will be run to the actual location of the home so that the final hookup can be done quickly and easily. Precise information should be available from the manufacturer.

The process of putting the mobile home on its supports, levelling, and making the hookups is called the "set-up." The work is usually done by the dealer from whom you purchased the home, but the CAS study notes that many dealers do not know how to do this properly and have not been trained for this purpose. A bad set-up can cause endless problems.

If you are buying land with a mobile home in mind, make sure that you will be permitted to erect this type of home in the community. A local lawyer or the local governing board can give an immediate answer.

In general, the farther away the community is from large metropolitan areas, the greater the likelihood that the community permits mobile homes. However, even though you may legally erect a mobile home in the community, you might be faced with a group of angry neighbors who do not want a mobile near their conventional homes, fearing, sometimes justifiably, that the mobile home's presence will lower real estate values.

Mobile homes sited on open lots (flat land without the screening offered by trees or shrubs) are more visible than units placed on well-landscaped land. However, the open

A development of mobile homes (SOLITUDE VILLAGE, HIGH BRIDGE, N.J.)

lot has the advantage of offering greater maneuverability for the trucks making deliveries of units. The owner of a lot with trees will have to clear an area large enough for the delivery truck to turn around and ample space so that the unit can be properly placed on its understructure. If possible, try to have the unit delivered in the spring, summer, or fall, to avoid the problems caused by snow and ice if you are sited in a cold climate.

At present there are about 24,000 mobile home parks in the United States. Park space close to metropolitan or recreational areas is more limited and more expensive than space elsewhere.

There are two kinds of parks, open and closed. The owner of an open park offers space to anyone. The owner of a closed park rents space only to those who buy their units from him, and he forces the owner of the unit to sell the home back to him at his own price. The closed park owner makes a bundle when he sells you the unit, gets a monthly rent for the entire time you live there, and then gets you again when you want to move. Avoid closed parks if at all possible. The FHA will not guarantee a mortgage on a mobile home in a closed park.

Park rents, in 1973, ranged from $35 to $100 per month. In addition, some parks also charge utility and maintenance fees above and beyond the rent. Rents and fees have undoubtedly risen since then. Renting a space is like renting an apartment; you have to find out about the lease, if any, and precisely what is and what is not covered by the monthly rent. Also, it is vital to find out what rights you, as a tenant, have in the event the park owner suddenly decides to raise the rent.

In some parks you may be forced to buy certain services—gas, oil, milk delivery, even home improvements—from the park owner at what may be inflated prices.

If you are still interested in parks, check a recent edition of *Woodall's Directory* (see bibliography), which can be bought in many bookstores or borrowed from libraries. The directory not only lists the parks, but rates them as well by its own standards. Of the nation's 24,000 installations, only 13,000 met the publication's criteria. *Woodall's* also lists those parks which sell or lease lots, parks which lease mobile homes, companies which move mobile homes, manufacturers, and articles of interest to mobile home dwellers. No matter the rating, visit the park, walk around it, and talk with residents other than the manager or owner.

Some parks offer extensive community facilities—laundry rooms, clubhouses, and swimming pools, for example. The management may also take care of lawn mowing, garbage removal, snow plowing, and other services. Make sure that the quoted rent includes services and use of facilities. Restrictions may also exist. Some parks do not accept families with children or pets. Others may segregate families with children to one area and retirees to another. Virtually all parks have rules and regulations. Read them carefully before signing anything; you may not be able to accept the rules.

Leases in mobile home parks are rare, and you may find yourself evicted summarily from a park, with your mobile home. In most cases, you are entirely at the mercy of the owner.

Those parks which rent mobile units offer an advantage, for you can have a test run to see if you like living in a mobile home, if you like living in a park, and if you like living in that part of the country, all without the financial burden of ownership.

Should you seek land or a park space? That depends on your needs, savings, and goals. If yours is a transient life-style, a park is best. If you stay put and have the cash for a down payment on a mobile home and land, perhaps land ownership is advantageous. Put another way, do you want to pay rent or pay off a loan for land and home? If privacy is a criterion, you had best start hunting for land, for parks are densely populated.

Choosing a Mobile Home

Cost, length, width, floor plan, decor, and the reputations of dealer and manufacturer are the critical points. Your pocketbook will define your financial limits; state road regulations will define the maximum size of the home you buy. Floor plan and decor are personal choices. The more anxious you may be to own a mobile home, the more untarnished the reputation of dealer and manufacturer will seem.

To help you make these decisions, each manufacturer supplies literature describing his products, with photographs of the interior and sometimes the exterior, a list of options, sometimes a price list, and a very sketchy specifications list. Selecting a unit can be like dinner in a Chinese restaurant: one from column A (the floor plan you like), one from column B (the interior "decor" package you like), and one from column C (the exterior you like). And you have a wealth of side orders—called options—to choose from.

Photographs in brochures are often shot from angles that make the interior spaces seem larger and more spacious than they are in fact. Many models in the photographs are seated, so as to make the ceilings appear to be higher than they are.

A word of caution: You may see a photograph of a specific decor package—Spanish, Tudor, early American, contemporary, Mediterranean—that you like. The photograph may have been taken in a model larger than the one you intend buying, so the spatial qualities may not be the same in your unit. At best, think of these photographs only as rough guides, rather than as absolutely true representations of what will be delivered. If at all possible, visit a model of the actual unit you plan to purchase.

The most important choice, as with any home, is the floor plan. Single-wide mobile floor plans are limited by the 12' or 14' width; like modular homes, double-wide units have greater flexibility because of their 24' to 28' widths. Additional space for single-wides can be provided by using a tip-out—a 4' to 5' deep and up to 12' long alcove which folds into the basic unit during transportation and then unfolds at the site. Slide-outs (sometimes called pull-outs or

roll-outs) are similar but larger—usually 7' deep and about 12' long. Tag units are about 10' to 12' feet deep and come in a variety of lengths, the most common of which is 32'. These options add living area and variety to the floor plan and help to somewhat alter the shoe-box shape of the single-wide mobile home. Tip-outs and slide-outs are factory installed; tag units are separate structures which are transported separately and are attached after the mobile home is in place. Tag units can be bought with the basic home or sometime later; they are also called "add-a-rooms." Tip-outs and slide-outs, however, must be ordered with the home. Coachmen Homes offers one of the most extensive lines of tag units, ranging from 12' × 23' to 12' × 49'.

A single-wide mobile with a tag unit for the entry

An artist's rendering of a single-wide mobile home with four slide-out units, two in the front and two in the back (CHAMPION HOME BUILDERS)

Interior of a single-wide mobile home with an alcove created by a slide-out, also called a "pull-out" (SCHULT HOME CORP.)

Floor Plans

·Single-wide units are similar in plan to railroad flats; they are one-room wide and have a front door near one end. The entrance usually leads directly into the living room or kitchen and a narrow hall leads to the bedrooms in the back.

Before looking at various floor plans, try to assess your own life-style, perhaps in conjunction with the floor plan checklists in the introduction. The selection of a plan should

be based also on the present and expected size of your family. Bear in mind that space is tight and a miscalculation about the number of rooms or room sizes may be harder to live with in a mobile home.

Because double-wide floor plans are virtually identical with modular floor plans, we will only discuss 12′ and 14′ single-wides. See the floor plans illustrated in the chapter on modular homes for an idea of what you can expect from a double-wide.

Mobile homes now on the market offer

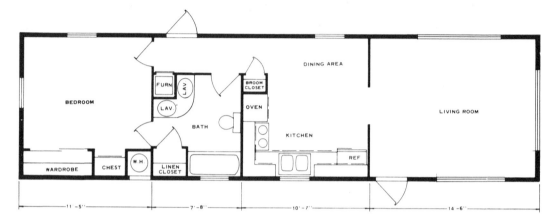

A one-bedroom single-wide mobile home floor plan (CONCHEMCO HOMES GROUP)

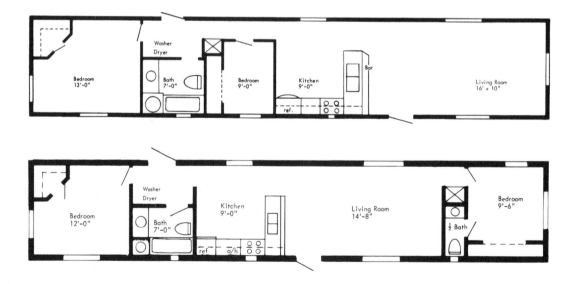

A two-bedroom single-wide back-to-back floor plan (top) *and a two-bedroom single-wide front bedroom floor plan* (bottom). *Both units have the same square footage* (PRICE-MEYERS CORPORATION)

from one to four bedrooms. The one-bedroom units are 50′ or less in length, while most four-bedroom mobiles are 70′ or more in length. The largest selection of models is within the two- and three-bedroom range, and a few manufacturers offer a two-bedroom unit in which one bedroom is sufficiently large to allow it to be partitioned into two bedrooms at some later date. Allocate one bedroom in the event you require a separate room for study or work, for it is not likely that you will find adequate space elsewhere in the mobile. The bedrooms are either back-to-back at one end of the house or are separated by the kitchen-living room area (a "front bedroom" model).

Kitchens are barely large enough for a small table and a few chairs or are simple working kitchens with the eating area in an adjacent room. Check the area of the kitchen carefully, for mobile homes have less in the way of working area and counter and storage space than other types of housing. Imagine yourself preparing dinner for four or baking a cake.

Floor plans are available with either the living room or kitchen at the front end of the home. Some manufacturers also offer one or more models with a small front room (perhaps as narrow as 6′ 6″) which is called a dining room or family room.

Plan your bathroom location carefully. If you have a front bedroom model, you might want a second full or half-bath at the front end of the house. Many manufacturers offer extra bathrooms and half-baths as options.

Almost all manufacturers offer clothes washing machines and dryers as options, while the necessary plumbing and electric wiring are part of the standard package. Laundry facilities are usually located in or in front of one of the bathrooms or in a small room off the kitchen. Exact location will be determined by the manufacturer's

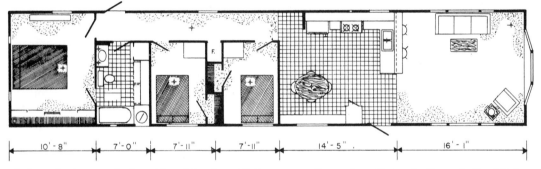

A three-bedroom single-wide with a front living room floor plan. Entry is through the kitchen (BONNAVILLA MOBILE HOME DIVISION OF CHIEF INDUSTRIES)

A three-bedroom single-wide with a front kitchen floor plan (GERRING INDUSTRIES)

*A three-bedroom single-wide with front living room and front hallway (*standard aisle*) (*top*) and a similar model with a rear hallway (*reverse aisle*). Both units have the same square footage* (DICKMAN HOMES)

floor plan, but if a laundry room is critical, you should shop around until you find the floor plan which best suits your needs.

Another factor is the location of hallways and, related to them, the location of a second door that leads to the outside. There are two basic designs; models with hallways running alongside the front of the house (sometimes called standard aisle) and models with hallways running along the rear of the house (sometimes called reverse aisle). "Front" and "rear" are determined by the location of the front door. The hallways are surprisingly narrow.

Mobile homes are required—as a safety precaution—to have a second door leading outside, and this door is usually off the hallway. A few floor plans include a third door, this one through the kitchen or from a small utility room off the kitchen at the rear of the house.

The location of hallways in conjunction with the siting of the unit will define the exposures of each of the rooms. Bear in mind that if you buy a mobile home with a specific

floor plan because you have a certain plot or park in mind, this floor plan may not serve the same function if the unit is moved elsewhere.

You will find, given the same area, that one manufacturer will have larger bedrooms and smaller living rooms and/or kitchens while another may reverse the proportions.

Here are the nine basic models carried by almost every manufacturer:

· Two-bedroom model with a front working kitchen and adjacent dinette area
· Two-bedroom model with front eat-in kitchen
· Two-bedroom model with front living room and two kitchen variants: an eat-in kitchen or a kitchen with an adjacent dinette
· Two-bedroom model with one bedroom in front and the living room next to that bedroom
· Two-bedroom model with a front den
· Three-bedroom model with a front working kitchen and adjacent dinette area

· Three-bedroom model with a front eat-in kitchen
· Three-bedroom model with a front living room and an eat-in kitchen or a working kitchen with an adjacent dinette area
· Three-bedroom model with one bedroom in front, next to the living room

Some manufacturers have a variety of models with some unusual features, while most offer only the basics as outlined above.

Lengths and Widths

Given the same area, a 14'-wide unit has rooms with better proportions than a 12'-wide unit. However, the 12'-wide allows more distance from one end of the home to the other. Here's an example of the same size house in different widths: a 67' x 12' (advertised as 70' by 12') has 804 square feet, while a 57' by 14' (advertised as a 60' by 14') has 798 square feet.

As of 1974, 39 states permitted 14'-wide units on their highways. Texas allows 16'-wide mobiles on its roads, but as of this writing it is the only state to do so. Until other states take a similar action, you would be limited to Texas with a 16'-wide.

Decor

A mobile home is a total living environment, fully furnished and decorated by the manufacturer. The decor package includes wall paneling (a thinner and cheaper substitute for wallboard), carpeting, vinyl flooring, furniture, curtains, appliances, electrical fixtures, and a slew of other accessories that may or may not be included in the base price (those accessories which are optional may be called an "optional decorator kit" or "decor package"). Some manufacturers go as far as offering optional bath towels that perfectly match their decor.

A typical assortment of furniture that is standard includes a kitchen (or dinette) table and four chairs, a sofa, one or more easy chairs, a table for the living room, and a bed and chest of drawers in each bedroom. Closets in all rooms are built-in.

Some floor plans show the location of furniture (it is by no means clear if the furniture has been drawn to scale by the manufacturer's artist), while others do not. Do your own drawings to scale of the floor plan and furniture if only to see exactly how much space your rooms will have once all of the furniture is in place. Use graph paper.

The quality of the furniture in the deluxe models is somewhat higher than the economy line equivalent. Try to find out—and it can be difficult with mobile manufacturers—just what you are getting in the way of woods, cloths, upholstery, and size. Though you might prefer buying your own furniture, be advised that the price discount given by the manufacturer to those who refuse the furnishings package is so low as to make it highly attractive to take the package. Better grade furniture, flooring, decor packages, and such are frequently available for additional cost. Some manufacturers of double-wides do not include furnishings in their base prices.

Generally, one has a choice of one of three or more decor packages. Among the most typical are Spanish (wrought iron fixtures, red and black upholstery, perhaps a picture of a bullfight on the wall), early American (colonial-style furniture, flowered upholstery, and an eagle wall plaque or two), and contemporary (simpler lines). Less common is a Greek decor package and one emulating the life-style of the Mediterranean, among others. All of them are designed to suit the tastes of the largest possible public.

Some manufacturers provide built-in furniture, which is quite sensible given the limited floor space. Typical built-in pieces are bedroom dressers (some companies offer free-standing dressers as options, considering them luxuries), bars, and space dividers. One company, Gerring Industries, can supply a built-in ironing board and a built-in desk, two good ideas.

Certain interior architectural features, sold as options, add some visual interest,

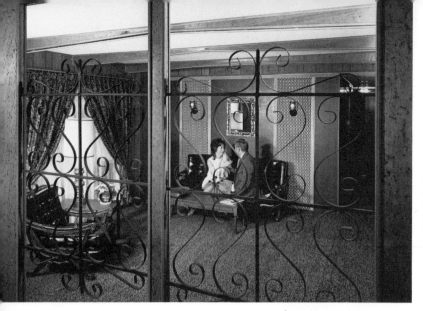

Interior of a mobile home living room with ornamental grill and decorative beams (CONCHEMCO HOMES GROUP)

Interior of a mobile home bedroom in traditional decor (MONARCH INDUSTRIES)

Interior of a mobile home with an eat-in kitchen (CHAMPION HOME BUILDERS)

such as raised ceilings over the living room (the standard 7′ ceiling might be too low for some), different levels between the living room, dining area, and/or kitchen formed by a platform, a bay window which is usually at the front end, and other items. These are often standard in the medium-priced or luxury lines.

Exterior

Except for units with tip-outs, slide-outs, or tag units, all single- and double-wide mobiles are pure rectangles. In many cases, the harsh metallic siding does little to detract from the plain shape. Two manufacturers, at this writing, produce units with wood siding, one is in California (Lakewood), the other in Wisconsin (Dickman).

Mobile homes have shallow-pitched roofs. A few manufacturers offer units with slightly greater pitches, which relieve the flat-roof look of mobile homes, but at best they do not approach the angle of the roof of stick-built homes. Others offer windows, fake shutters, and doors that are very similar to those used on conventional homes, and some provide horizontal aluminum siding which simulates clapboard.

In many mobile homes small windows are installed higher off the floor than those of conventional housing. Although this may be attractive and it also allows for better use of the limited wall space, the higher the window is off the floor the harder it is to use as an exit in the event of fire. You may be able to have the windows lowered by the manufacturer, and you may be able to order larger windows as options.

Perhaps the one way to make the exterior more closely resemble a traditional home is to use a tip-out, slide-out, or tag unit which will break up the box-like appearance of the unit while adding additional space. More help would come from adding a porch, patio, deck, trellis, or anything that visually ties the mobile home to its site.

One manufacturer, National Homes, aware of the need to improve the exterior appearance of mobile homes, commissioned the Frank Lloyd Wright Foundation to design several units. A prototype model from the design project was shown in one of the company's annual reports. Judging by this model, the design helped to alleviate the stark rectangular shape. However, the Wright Foundation design is not in production.

The Wright Foundation also did a study for the Wisconsin Department of Natural Resources of ways in which mobile and modular homes could be designed to blend with the natural landscape. They developed a number of interesting designs based on Wright's idea of "opening up the box." You can't buy one, of course, because no one is making them.

There is a clear need for more attractive mobile home exterior design, and it is too bad that first efforts were aborted.

Landscaping

Landscaping for mobile homes, on private land or in a park, is particularly important. The excellent advice given below, though intended primarily for mobile home owners, is applicable to anyone building any kind of home. The quotation and illustrations are drawn from "Landscaping the Mobile Home," by Craig S. Oliver, Professor of Ornamental Horticulture at Pennsylvania State University (see Bibliography).

Today, the mobile home community presents a new concept of living for many families. The well-designed community includes an abundance of open space as an integral part of living space surrounding the individual mobile home. For you, the mobile home owner, the greenery of plants throughout the community and within the confines of your property boundaries creates a pleasant, individualized, and functional setting. . . .

Basically, what you do will depend entirely upon your desires and interest in outdoor gardening. But, regardless of what you decide, the basic design

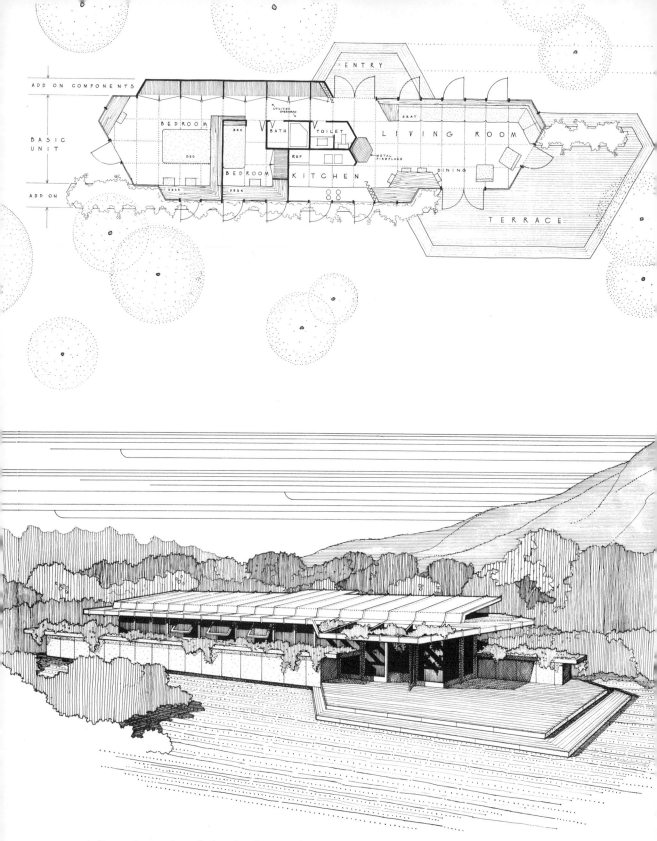

A floor plan and rendering by the Frank Lloyd Wright Foundation of what a mobile home can look like. The unusual angled walls are intended as pull-outs which would be stored within the home during transportation. The floor plan also shows a metal fireplace, which is not available in mobile homes today. It could be factory produced; it would not be inexpensive, for no good design is cheap (FRANK LLOYD WRIGHT FOUNDATION © 1970)

should be simple, attractive, and functional.

Too many plants are as bad as none at all. Before planting trees or shrubs, determine where they are needed. Possibly a few shrubs along the foundation, a tree near the patio, or annual flowers along the entry wall will suffice. . . .

The smaller the ground surrounding the mobile home, the greater the need for proper planting. . . . Plants that you desire to include in your landscaped setting can be indicated directly on the plan (of your land and the precise location of your home) you have prepared. During the planning process, circles or squares can be drawn on the plan where you feel plants should be located. These circles or squares should be indicated (in scale) at the eventual spread a plant will reach at maturity. Using this technique will help you determine how much space each plant will take and whether plants are located too close together. . . .

The general rule to remember in placing plants in the landscape is that the spread of a plant is usually equal to its eventual height. Learn the mature spread of a plant and then space each plant at least one-half the total spread away from the house or from another plant. This will provide space for it to develop without interference. . . .

Tall-growing shrubs can be used at the corners of the home where the windows are not located. Plants used in this manner help to accent the home and create a pleasing transition between the horizontal ground line and the vertical lines of the house.

One or two medium- to low-growing trees may also be of benefit in the landscape setting. A properly placed tree can frame the house, shade the patio, and provide an attractive accent from both within and outdoors.

All plants have specific soil requirements that must be considered when selecting shrubs and trees for the home grounds. Soil modification at planting time is usually necessary if you wish to balance air and water for good plant growth. In addition, minimum winter temperatures and exposed locations subjected to wind will affect plant selection. It is important to determine the relative hardiness of a plant to these conditions if you wish success in growing plants.

Before purchasing plants, ask your local nurseryman or county agricultural agent for specific information about plant hardiness or special cultural requirements. They will be happy to assist you with information to fill your individual needs.

We would also recommend *Taylor's Encyclopedia of Gardening,** which describes the hardiness of trees and shrubs as well as offering guidelines to heights and widths. Professor Oliver continues:

(1) Taller plants should be used at the corners of the home. (2) Don't overplant. Be sure you know the ultimate size of each plant and allow for growth. (3) Balance is important in landscaping. Don't have one area of your property a lot more colorful or more heavily planted than another. (4) Be sure to select plants that are known to grow well in your area. (5) Scale is important. Don't plant trees and shrubs that grow too tall. (6) To make people feel welcome to your home, don't place large shrubs near the door. (7) Space plants far enough apart so you don't have to prune excessively. (8) Keep planting simple and attractive. (9) It is not always necessary to hide the whole foundation of the home with shrubs. Ground covers used in spaces between plants will tie the plantings together. (10) Plants selected and used properly have many functional values. They can block unsightly views, modify the climate, and direct people to areas you wish to emphasize."

* Boston: Houghton Mifflin Company.

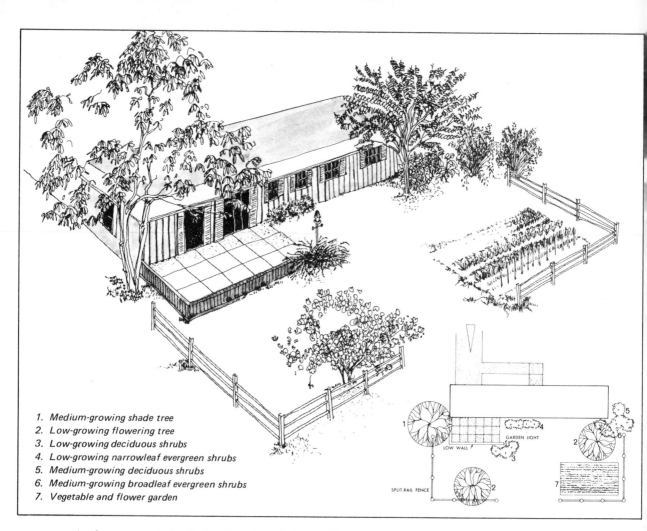

1. *Medium-growing shade tree*
2. *Low-growing flowering tree*
3. *Low-growing deciduous shrubs*
4. *Low-growing narrowleaf evergreen shrubs*
5. *Medium-growing deciduous shrubs*
6. *Medium-growing broadleaf evergreen shrubs*
7. *Vegetable and flower garden*

A pleasant and simple landscaping design with a patio and vegetable garden, and trees for shade. Some may not find the need for two fences in so small an area: a split-rail fence and a low fence enclosing the patio (CRAIG S. OLIVER)

Landscaping is fun, enhances daily living, increases the value of your property, and complements your home.

Mobile Home Construction

Efficient factory production and lower-grade materials are two of the principal aspects leading to the low cost of mobile homes. The materials are characterized as lower-grade in comparison with all other forms of housing; yet they are quite a bit better today than they were in the industry's early days. And today most companies follow an industry-wide code, which has also been adopted by most states and those federal agencies which guarantee loans to mobile home buyers.

When you price mobile homes, bear in mind that most manufacturers provide the same construction materials in all of their units, be they in the economy, mid-range, or luxury lines. The line is defined primarily by the extras—the "flash" and pizzazz—rather than by a better-built structure. Or, put simpler, each unit, regardless of line, is as structurally sound as the others.

The level of information offered by manufacturers in their specifications lists varies from useful to useless, and the mobile home people are more reluctant than other manufacturers to tell the buyer exactly what he is getting. We have already commented on

1. *Low-growing flowering tree*
2. *Low-growing narrowleaf evergreen*
3. *Medium-growing deciduous shrubs*
4. *Low-growing evergreen or deciduous shrubs*
5. *Ground cover*
6. *Medium-growing broadleaf evergreen shrubs*

In this design, the piers or pads of the mobile are hidden from view by low and medium growing shrubbery (CRAIG S. OLIVER)

the reasons for this reticence. Some examples of what you might come across are "a superb refrigerator-freezer ample for a hungry family," which is not as informative as saying "14 (or 12 or 16) cubic-foot refrigerator-freezer"; "more than adequate insulation to keep you comfortable all year" is not conducive to letting you compare this manufacturer's insulation with that of one of his competitors, nor is it as useful as an R rating (see the specifications chapter, the section on insulation) or naming the kind of insulation used with a thickness-in-inches reference.

Actual specifications may vary from company to company, and you may find that one product is sturdier than another. You might also find it useful to read the specifications chapter, where for various components of a house are compared for mobile, modular, and prefabricated homes.

Costs

This is the only area where mobile homes offer real appeal. The quoted price can be very attractive.

Start calculating with the base cost of the unit. Add to that all options and whatever taxes may be applicable.

A word about options. We envision the day tires will be options on automobiles. The mobile home manufacturers have such an option. It is called a "site preparation option" and consists of skirting, anchoring, steps, and piers, of which all but skirting are absolutely essential to the preparation of the home. Skirting is useful to hide and protect the wheels of the chassis. These options may add 15% of the base cost to your total cash outlay.

Add to this the cost of transportation to the site, hook-up fees at a mobile home park, or the additional expenses incurred if you purchase land (cost, legal fees, taxes, installation of services, land preparation, hook-ups).

Basic costs vary widely depending upon size, manufacturer, and extras. Even for mobile homes of the same size, there can be substantial price differences. A few years ago one of the most popular sizes was 12' x 65' (about 744 square feet without the hitch) and you could buy a unit of this size from one manufacturer for $8,000 in the economy line, $9,000 in the midrange line, or $10,000 in the deluxe line.

According to one industry source, the average cost of a single-wide unit in 1973 was $7,770; the lowest price we saw quoted was $3,500 for a 40' x 12' (really 37' x 12' without the hitch) stripped-down economy model. The same manufacturer also sold a 64' x 24' (really 61' x 24') double-wide in his luxury line for $25,000. The $3,500 unit averaged $7.88 per square foot; the $25,000 unit was $17.07 per square foot and was loaded with extras.

Useful, but not vital, options include carport, garage, patio, porch or screened room, awnings, trash stand, and utility shed. Remember that mobile homes do not have basements or extra storage spaces, so equipment or machinery that needs enclosed storage must be placed in a separate structure.

Then there are the interior extras, including appliances (fancier or larger than standard), fixtures, doors and windows (nicer or better than standard), furnishings, and additional insulation. Some itemized options lists have more than 100 details, such as bay windows, storm windows, 200-ampere electrical service. all-electric homes, additional

or more deluxe furniture, larger beds (which reduce the already limited bedroom floor space), better carpeting, larger furnace, larger capacity water heater or one with a quick recovery system, air conditioning, door chimes, or a removable hitch. If you select many of these options, you will leave the basic economy of mobile homes far behind.

Manufacturers will generally quote a mileage charge to transport the mobile to its site, but this amount does not include tolls, road permit fees charged by states, if any, or the cost of a flag car to accompany the truck if needed. Get a firm price for transportation from the dealer or manufacturer. Mileage costs in 1973 ranged from $.40 to $1.00 per mile per unit (double this rate for double-wides, which come on two trucks). Some manufacturers have a sliding scale depending upon the length of the unit, while others have a flat rate per mile per unit.

There are other cost factors, too. Are local taxes levied on mobile homes? State taxes? Licensing and inspection fees? Personal property taxes?

Buying a Mobile Home

Mobile homes are usually bought from a local dealer, who may also be the owner of a mobile home park. Manufacturers will usually send lists of their dealers. Bear in mind that the average selling territory is about 300 miles from the plant. The larger manufacturers have plants in different parts of the country, and even though their address for information may be in, say California, they may have a plant in New England.

Another point to consider is the length of time a manufacturer has been in business. There are many business failures among manufacturers of mobile, modular, and prefabricated homes. It may be more advantageous to buy from a long-established firm, even if the unit is more expensive, to have a continuity of service and parts.

The CAS study claims that the relationship between dealer and manufacturer is tenuous at best, hinging only on the amount of capital the dealer may have for his business. Manufacturers set no standards for their dealers, nor do they offer training or supervision. Almost anyone with capital can become a mobile home dealer. Hopefully, you will find an honest and competent dealer.

The dealer serves three functions: he sells the unit, he supervises the set-up on site, and he services the unit, fulfilling the terms of the warranty (which may range from 90 days to one year). Warranties and guarantees are only as good as the people behind them. CAS has charged that many dealers and manufacturers pass the buck to each other when it comes to repairs, and it is the consumer who suffers. And manufacturers will sometimes refuse to make repairs unless the home is returned to the factory! Not only do you pay the transportation costs back and forth, but you also have to find a place to live until the manufacturer gets around to fulfilling his obligation.

Furthermore, many dealers may be one-man operations, with no trained repairmen available for service. Until some form of national standards are adopted and properly enforced, the most the buyer can do is pray that the dealer will do what must be done.

Before signing anything, find out if the manufacturer is a member of the major trade association, the Mobile Homes Manufacturers Association/Trailer Coach Association. The MHMA people are east of the Rockies, TCA members are west. MHMA/TCA may help with your problems with the manufacturer.

The association was instrumental in developing a construction code through the American National Standards Institute (ANSI) which is called ANSI-A 119.1. Though ANSI sounds like a governmental agency, it is not; it is privately owned and operated. To date, 46 states have adopted ANSI-A 119.1, so membership in MHMA/TCA is not critical if you are concerned about enforcement of the code.

A code, like warranties or guarantees, is only good if it is enforced. CAS reports that

MHMA/TCA had 14 inspectors in a field of 500 factories producing 400,000 units a year, which is not impressive from the consumer protection point of view. Some states have their own inspection forces, which probably do a more thorough job than the tiny MHMA/TCA staff.

ANSI-A 119.1 is a performance code, not a construction code. It does not tell manufacturers what materials should be used or how the mobile home should be built; it only tells the manufacturer that a certain performance minimum must be provided. It covers body, frame, heating, plumbing, and the electrical system. CAS charges that the code is not as strong as it might be and that it has not solved the very basic problems of fire retardation and preventing mobiles from being blown over by high winds.

In addition, ANSI-A 119.1 requires that a certificate be posted in the mobile home specifying the minimum climactic conditions which the home and furnace will meet (i.e., lowest outdoor temperature at a given wind velocity), the "structural zone" of the country for which the home was designed (a unit intended for Florida might not do very well in Nebraska in January), and for homes in hurricane zones, a diagram showing where tie-down anchors are to be positioned. CAS has also charged that the present anchoring system is not adequate.

Finance

This is a particularly problematical area. Many banks and savings and loan associations consider mobile homes as vehicles rather than as houses, because they are easily moved, have a shorter life span than a permanently installed, better built home on a foundation, and because they depreciate with time. As a result, lending institutions generally grant personal loans rather than long-term mortgages to mobile home purchasers.

You will generally have less than ten years to repay the principal and interest when you buy a mobile home. Personal loans for the purchase of mobile homes have variable interest rates depending on the amount borrowed; the lower the amount, the lower the interest rate may be. Interest rates are set by state banking commissions—that is, maximum rates are specified by law (this does not prevent some lending institutions from charging less than the legal maximum).

Here is a comparison for the buyer of a mobile home and a buyer of a modular, prefabricated, or stick-built home who needs $10,000. The interest rates quoted were prevalent in New Jersey when the book was written. The relationships between personal loan and mortgage rates would be about the same throughout the country, though the actual interest rates may vary.

Mobile buyer: $10,000 at 10 years personal loan at 8% (the maximum bank rate allowed by New Jersey law) interest—120 payments of $121.33 for a total of $14,-559.60, or $4,559.60 in interest (46% of the amount borrowed).

Modular, prefabricated, or stick-built home buyer: $10,000 at 10 years at 9% interest—120 payments of $126.68 for a total of $15,201.60, or $5,201.60 in interest (52% of the amount borrowed). Or $10,-000 at 20 years at 9% interest—240 payments of $89.98 for a total of $21,595.20, or $11,595.20 in interest (115% of the amount borrowed). Or $10,000 at 25 years at 9% interest—300 payments of $83.92 for a total of $25,176.00, or $15,176.00 in interest (152% of the amount borrowed). Or $10,000 at 30 years at 9% interest—360 payments of $80.47 for a total of $28,-969.20, or $18,969.20 in interest (190% of the amount borrowed).

The cost of money is not the same everywhere. While maximum interest rates for lending institutions are set by the states, you might be able to find a bank (commercial or savings) or savings and loan association that will lend at a lower rate. But the rate alone is not the only information you need, for some banks who may charge lower interest rates may also tack on various other charges —points, application fees, inspection fees— which when added to the total interest paid over the course of the loan may bring the actual interest rate paid up to that of other banks. There is competition but the range of saving is narrow.

You can finance your home through the dealer. His interest rates and various fees may not be regulated by the state and, consequently, may be very high indeed. Dealers generally require less of a down payment than lending institutions to encourage sales and to encourage the buyer to finance his mobile home through the dealer.

The cost of money from a dealer is almost always higher than from a lending institution, because the dealer is himself borrowing money from the institution and then lending it to you. As a result, you are paying the dealer for his interest, which he pays the lender, plus, as always, a profit. And the dealer may quote what sounds like a favorable interest rate but it really is an add-on rate. A "7% add-on" rate equals 12.6% in real interest. In New Jersey dealers can charge as much as 10% add-on.

Here is the difference between simple and add-on interest rates. We'll deal with $10,-000 for 10 years. You receive $10,000 in cash when you sign the note. Of each monthly payment you make, in a simple interest situation, like a mortgage, a certain amount of that payment is applied to reducing the $10,000 borrowed, while the balance of the payment is interest. Therefore, your first installment includes interest on $10,000; your second installment will include interest on the $10,000 less whatever of your first installment was applied to the amount borrowed, and so on. Though the amount of your monthly payment remains the same, the balance between interest and principal changes. As more money is applied to principal, less money is paid in interest.

Add-on interest is quite different and more expensive. If you borrow $10,000 for 10 years, you pay the stated interest rate on the full $10,000 for the full 10 years. Now you can see why 7% add-on will total a lot more money than 9% simple interest.

We do not mean to imply that dealers are the only ones charging add-on interest. In New Jersey, banks and savings and loan associations offering personal loans under

$5,500 can quote up to 6% add-on, which is 11.25% true interest, but probably still less than the add-on rates charged by dealers.

Depreciation is a complicating factor in financing a mobile home. The Center for Auto Safety estimates 50% depreciation in five years. Mobiles depreciate while other forms of housing appreciate. Depreciation is especially difficult in inflationary times, because a used mobile home will be sold for fewer dollars, each of which is worth less than the dollar used to buy the unit initially. They may depreciate even more if they are moved frequently, because of the possibility of damage to the structural soundness.

The New Building Block, a book dealing with a Cornell University study, estimates that mobile housing has a 15 to 20 year life, whereas other forms of housing have a life span of 50 years and up.

In the short run, mobile housing is cheapest of all. In the long run, it may well prove to be the most expensive form of housing.

A word about mobile home insurance. Many dealers will try to sell you insurance at inflated rates and may offer, under the guise of better serving you, to include the cost of insurance in your monthly payments if he, the dealer, is also financing the unit. There is no reason why you should not buy mobile home insurance from an insurance broker, probably at lower rates than offered by the dealer. However, you may be in for a surprise when you see these "lower" rates, which will be higher than insurance rates for all other forms of housing. Mobile homes are charged higher rates because of the possibility of a fire doing greater damage in a mobile than in other forms of housing.

Caveat emptor is the best advice we can give the potential mobile home buyer.

Buying a Used Mobile Home

This is your best buy. By the time you buy a used mobile home, most of the high depreciation will have been the burden of the original owner. The purchaser of a used mobile home usually takes possession of all furnishings as well, and these show wear and tear very clearly. You should not expect otherwise, considering the generally low level of materials used by the manufacturers. A used mobile is far less than a new one in cost and can be especially attractive for people on very tight budgets.

You can find used mobiles in a number of ways: newspaper advertisements, dealer trade-ins, owners of mobile homes who have units for sale, or real estate brokers. No matter who sells you a used mobile home, we strongly recommend that you hire a professional engineer or a reputable mobile home repairman to give the used home a once-over to make sure there are no serious problems.

Like the used car market, the used mobile home market has its source for "book value." It is called the *Blue Book* (see bibliography) and is published three times a year. It lists average prices of mobile homes by manufacturer and model.

One cautionary note about used mobile homes. Some standards and specifications, especially those that result from a documented attack on the industry, like the Center of Auto Safety study, are subject to upgrading. The buyer of a used mobile home will not benefit from these changes, some of which may be absolutely vital for safety.

Manufacturers

Here is a list of those manufacturers who responded to our inquiries. All manufacture 12'-wides and some, as noted below, make 14'-wides. Most manufacturers sell a variety of models in a number of different lines, all of which change from year to year, though the basic materials and floor plans may remain constant. "Standard floor plans" refers to the basic floor plans described earlier. Variants are described here. We have not attempted to list all of the lines because they are too numerous. Even though a manufacturer has plants all over the country, he may manufacture the model you want in a plant very distant from your site, and you might not be able to get it. Other companies are mentioned in industry lists available to the public (see Bibliography).

BELLAVISTA-BONNAVILLA (Chief Industries, Box 288, Aurora, Nebraska 68818) markets its units west of the Mississippi, including Mississippi but excluding the West Coast and Idaho; manufactures 14'-wides and double-wides; standard floor plans and units with a center family room.

BENDIX HOME SYSTEMS, INC. (61 Perimeter Park East, Atlanta, Georgia 30341) markets units throughout the country; 14'-wides and double-wides; large variety of floor plans for both single- and double-wide homes including a one-bedroom unit and a floor plan with a large front bedroom that can be made into two rooms.

CHAMPION HOME BUILDERS (5573 E. North Street, Dryden, Michigan 48428) markets units throughout the country; 14'-wides and double-wides; slide-outs available; two-bedroom units with front bedroom and kitchen and a three-bedroom unit with a front bedroom and kitchen, as well as standard floor plans.

COACHMEN HOMES (P.O. Box 612, Middlebury, Indiana 46540) markets units in the midwest, New England, and New York; single- and double-wides; tip-outs, slide-outs, and a large selection of tag units; two-bedroom units having front bedroom and kitchen, three-bedroom model with front dining room or den; and four-bedroom units available as well as standard floor plans.

CONCHEMCO HOMES GROUP (P.O. Box 2078, Shawnee Mission, Kansas 66201) markets units nationwide; 14'-wides and double-wides; offers a one-bedroom unit and a three-bedroom unit with front dining room or den as well as standard floor plans.

CRAFTMADE HOMES (P.O. Box 388, Sylvester, Georgia 31791) markets units in Georgia; offers one- and four-bedroom plans in addition to standard floor plans.

DeROSE INDUSTRIES (4002 Meadows Drive, Indianapolis, Indiana 46205) did not specify its marketing area; plants in Pennsylvania, North Carolina, Georgia, Indiana, Michigan, Texas, and Minnesota; 16'-wides for Texas as well as 14'-wides and double-wides; slide-outs; standard floor plans.

DICKMAN HOMES (P.O. Box 93, Spencer, Wisconsin 54479) markets units in north central states; only manufactures 14'-wide units; offers three bedroom units with front bedroom and kitchen in addition to standard floor plans; offers a wood siding option; high quality construction by mobile home standards.

DMH CO. (1517 Virginia Street, St. Louis, Michigan 48880) did not specify its marketing area; plants in Pennsylvania, Georgia, Michigan, Minnesota, Kansas, and California; offers 14'-wides and double-wide units; slide-outs; two-bedroom model with front bedroom and kitchen, three-bedroom model with front dining room or den, and four-bedroom units; a model with a large bedroom which can be divided into two rooms, and standard floor plans.

GERRING INDUSTRIES (Shipshewana, Indiana 46565) markets units in the East, central states, midwest, and Florida; 14'-wides and double-wides; offers a one-bedroom unit in addition to standard floor plans; tip-outs and slide-outs.

HERRLI INDUSTRIES (2801 Oakland Avenue, P.O. Box 848, Elkhart, Indiana 46514) markets units in the East, midwest, and Canada; 14'-wides and double-wides; offers a one-bedroom unit in addition to standard floor plans; tip-outs, slide-outs, and tag units.

LAKEWOOD INDUSTRIES (18026 South Broadway, Gardena, California 90248) markets units throughout the country; primarily manufactures double-wides and offers some 20'-wide units; offers wood siding; a one-bedroom unit as well as standard floor plans are available.

MANSION HOMES (P.O. Box 756, Robbins, North Carolina 27325) markets units from Pennsylvania to South Carolina;

offers a three-bedroom unit with front dining room or den and a four-bedroom model
in addition to standard floor plans.

MARLETTE HOMES (Lewistown,
Pennsylvania 17044) did not specify marketing area; plants in Pennsylvania, Georgia,
Michigan, Kansas, Oregon, and Ontario;
standard floor plans; tip-outs, tag-units;
double-wides.

MIDLAND COMPANY (First National
Bank Building, Cincinnati, Ohio 45202)
markets units in the midwest, mid-Atlantic
states, and southeast; 14'-wides and double-
wides; offers two- and three-bedroom units
with front bedroom and kitchen and standard floor plans.

MONARCH INDUSTRIES (P.O. Box
1, Goshen, Indiana 46526) did not specify
marketing area; plants in Indiana, Georgia,
and North Carolina; 14'-wides and double-
wides; an unusually large number of floor
plans, including a one-bedroom unit and a
three-bedroom unit with front dining room
or den; tag units.

PRICE-MEYERS CORP. (P.O. Box 36,
1135 Kent Street, Elkhart, Indiana 46514)
did not specify marketing area; plants in
Pennsylvania, Indiana, North Carolina, and
Texas; 14'-wides; offers three-bedroom
model with front dining room or den in addition to standard floor plans; tip-outs and
slide-outs.

REDMAN MOBILE HOMES (7800
Carpenter Freeway, Dallas, Texas 75247)
markets units throughout the country; 16
plants; 14'-wides and double-wides; large
selection of floor plans.

REPUBLIC HOMES (P.O. Box 401,
Laurens, South Carolina 29360) markets
units in North and South Carolina, Tennes-
see, and Virginia; standard floor plans.

SCHULT HOME CORP. (P.O. Box 359,
Edwardsburg, Michigan 49112) did not specify marketing area; plants in Indiana, Maryland, Michigan, Kansas, Kentucky, Florida,
Ohio, and Texas; offers standard floor plans
and a three-bedroom model with front dining room or den; 14'-wides and double-
wides; tip-outs and slide-outs.

TOWN & COUNTRY MOBILE HOMES
(P.O. Box 5003, Wichita Falls, Texas

76307) markets units in the southwest,
south central states, and southeast; 14'-wides
with one unit 80' in length; standard floor
plans and a three-bedroom model with a
front bedroom-sitting room, a three-bedroom model with a front bedroom and
kitchen, and a model with an "upper-level"
(somewhat raised) bedroom in the front.

Cost Checklist

The list which follows is designed to help
you calculate what your costs will be and to
help you make valid comparisons between
different manufacturers and models. We
recommend that you make a copy of these
pages and answer all questions for each
model you are considering. Comparing all
of the completed checklists should indicate,
roughly, which manufacturer is offering the
better price. The cost checklist should be
used in conjunction with the materials checklist at the end of the specifications chapter.

Mobile Home Erected on Land Owned by the Purchaser

1. The Building Lot

Land $_____
Lawyer (including all contracts
  for land and home, searches,
  closing, and anticipated ap-
  pearances before local
  boards) $_____
Land survey (if recent survey
  unavailable from seller) $_____
Title insurance (one-time ex-
  pense) $_____
Land transfer taxes, if any $_____
Building permit application fee $_____
Building permit $_____
Soil percolation test (if you are
  installing a septic system) $_____
Soil log (for septic system) $_____
Engineered septic design $_____
Septic system permit $_____
Well permit (if you have to dig
  your own well) $_____

2. The Mobile Home

Mobile home basic package $_____
Floor plan modification(s) $_____
Options (itimize) _____
_____ $_____
Transportation to site and set-up $_____
Total payment due dealer or
  manufacturer $_____
Taxes, if any, on purchase price $_____
Other necessary buildings (ga-
  rage, carport, storage sheds,
  etc.) $_____
Other exterior construction
  (stairs, skirting, patio, deck,
  etc.) $_____

3. Site work

Land clearing, if necessary, to
  receive the mobile home $_____
Preliminary grading $_____
Foundation, pads, or piers $_____
Road or driveway construction $_____
Road or driveway surface
  (stone, macadam) $_____
Installation of above-ground
  electric service $_____
  or
Installation of underground
  electric service $_____
If underground and you pay for
  the trench, how much? $_____
If a transformer is required and
  you pay for it, how much? $_____
If the transformer requires a pad
  and you pay for it, how
  much? $_____
Electrical hookup from service $_____
line to home $_____
Installation of above-ground
  telephone service $_____
  Will the telephone company
  allow you to install underground service in the same
  trench with underground
  electric service?
Telephone installation (equipment, receivers, service
  charge) $_____

Septic system built to prevailing
  specifications or better $_____
Plumbing and hookup from
  septic system to home $_____
  or
Plumbing and hookup from
  home to existing public
  sewerage lines $_____
Cased-in well dug to prevailing
  specifications or better and
  desired water pressure $_____
Plumbing and hookup from
  well to home $_____
  or
Plumbing and hookup from
  public water supply to home $_____
Final grading $_____
Inspections $_____
Occupancy permit $_____

4. Other Expenses

Homeowner's insurance policy
  on the home per year (usually
  required by the lending institution) $_____
Budget for landscaping per year
  (lawn, trees, shrubs, etc.) $_____
Estimated annual property taxes $_____
Other annual municipal taxes $_____

Mobile Home in a Mobile Home Park

1. The Park

Monthly rental for space in the
  park $_____
  Is the park "open" or
  "closed"?
Hookups for services if not included within the monthly
  rental $_____
Use of all facilities within the
  park if not included within
  the monthly rental $_____
Lawyer (to review contracts of
  the dealer and/or manu-
  facturer and all documents
  dealing with renting space in
  the park) $_____

2. The Mobile Home

Mobile home basic package $_____
Floor plan modification(s) $_____
Options (itimize) _____
_____ $_____
Transportation to site and set-up $_____
Total payment due dealer or manufacturer $_____
Taxes, if any, on purchase price $_____
Other necessary buildings (garage, carport, storage sheds, etc.) $_____
Other exterior construction (stairs, skirting, patio, deck, etc.) $_____

3. Other Expenses

Homeowner's insurance policy on the home per year (usually required by the lending institution) $_____
Estimate your annual maintenance costs (painting, cleaning, general repairs) $_____

Utilities

Estimate your monthly electric bill $_____
Estimate your monthly gas bill $_____
Estimate your monthly fuel (for heating) bill $_____
Estimate your monthly telephone bill $_____
Estimate your monthly garbage collection bill if not provided for the landowner by the municipality or for the renter by the park management $_____
Estimate your annual bill for use of public sewerage lines $_____
Estimate your annual bill for use of public water supply $_____

Money

How much money will you need? $_____

How much money do you have? $_____
How much of the cash you have in hand will you be applying as a down payment on the mobile home? $_____
How large a loan will you need? $_____
For how many years (when they tell you the monthly payment you'll know how long a period you'll need)?
For lending institutions (commercial banks, savings banks, and savings and loan associations):
Will you borrow the amount as a personal loan or mortgage?
At what interest rate? (% per year) ____%
Is the interest rate "simple interest" or "add-on interest"?
If add-on interest, what is the "true interest" rate? (% per year) ____%
If the lending institution charges a fee for processing your loan or mortgage application, how much? $_____
If the lending institution charges "points," how much will this cost? $_____
Are there any other one-time fees or charges levied by the institution and how much will they cost? $_____
Does the lending institution penalize you for the early repayment of the loan? If so, what is the penalty? $_____
For dealer financing: As the interest rate quoted is generally "add-on," what is the true interest rate? (% per year) ____%
What is the term of the dealer's loan? (years)
Does the dealer charge any fees above and beyond the add-on interest and, if so, how much and for what? $_____

Does the monthly payment to the lending institution or the dealer include all municipal taxes, if any?

What is the total amount of money you will pay for your loan (the number of installments multiplied by the monthly payment)? $_____

Of this amount, how much is interest and fees (deduct the principal borrowed from the total amount of money you pay the lending institution)? $_____

MODULAR HOUSES

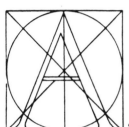 "module" in its contemporary sense is an element, a unit, which when attached to other similar units forms a complete living habitat. The term has come to mean a "box" with all of the necessary ingredients installed at a plant or factory and which, when placed on a permanent foundation, is ready for immediate occupancy.

Here are some of the advantages of modular homes:

1. *Cost.* In general, given the same square footage, modular homes are less expensive than prefabricated homes, though more expensive than mobile homes.

2. *On-site labor.* Modulars, like prefabricated homes and unlike mobile homes, require the on-site construction of a foundation. Other than rough plumbing and provision for services, there is very little other on-site work.

3. *Appreciation.* Whereas mobile homes depreciate, modular homes, like prefabricated and stick-built homes, appreciate.

4. *Financing.* Modulars, because they are permanent structures which are not moved once they have been set on their foundation, are financed by conventional long-term mortgages.

5. *Appearance.* Because of their more conventional pitched roofs and proportions, modulars look more like conventionally built homes than many mobile homes (double-wide mobiles, however, look very much like modulars).

6. *Range of styles.* One can buy a one-story ranch (the most common style), two-story, bi-level, or A-frame modular home.

7. *Suitability for level or sloping ground.* Modular and prefabricated homes can be located on level or sloping ground, unlike mobile homes which require level ground for their pads or piers.

8. *Floor plan flexibility.* You can make more floor plan changes of modular homes than mobile homes but fewer changes than prefabricated homes.

9. *Code conformity.* A modular home stands a much better chance of conforming to prevailing codes than mobile homes, because modular homes are built better, with higher grade materials.

Modular homes also have drawbacks, and here are the two basic ones:

1. *Design limitations.* Modulars are virtually all 24′ in width to avoid problems of transporting the two halves of the house over public highways, and they tend to look like boxes. But A-frames and bi-levels offer a respite. These design limitations, in our view, are not inherent in the technology but are forced upon the public by manufacturers who offer no alternatives.

2. *Code conformity.* Because they are constructed in a factory far from the on-site

supervision of a local building inspector, modular units may not pass a local building code. Building codes require the inspector to watch every facet of construction, and, clearly, a factory-built product cannot come under this step-by-step scrutiny.

In the most strikingly handsome modular structure of recent times, architect Moshe Safdie's Habitat in Montreal, individual modules were built at a nearby plant and then transported to the site where they were either attached on their sides or stacked. Habitat, we should point out, is a multi-storied apartment dwelling. Actually, it would more properly be called a living environment since the structure and grounds are far more complex than a house. Its residents are upper middle class and upper class and are able to pay high rents, resulting from the fact that Habitat was a prototype, and could not achieve the economies of very large scale mass production.

Writing about Habitat, Safdie offered the following lucid rationale behind the need for manufactured housing:

> While we were designing the Habitat interiors, I flew down to Toronto to see the Frigidaire assembly line. Since Frigidaire were going to build the Habitat kitchens, they wanted me to see the way they should be assembled so this could be taken into account in the design.
>
> It was enlightening. Here was a relatively complex product, a refrigerator, and yet it was assembled simply with few steps. The installing of a particular piece of insulant piping or wiring was timed to the second. Just compare that with a building site! Imagine an automobile assembly line where each step along the line is undertaken by a different company with its own financial interest and separate labor union! I'm convinced that no one is going to be able to mass produce a house until the entire process is under a single corporate structure, and probably a single union, too. Yet factory-made mass-produced housing is the magic word being whispered as the key to salvation.
>
> Present practice is impossible. The client asks an architect to design something specifically for him. In making drawings the architect will specify various components out of catalogues. He is nearly always restricted to elements that are already manufactured. Then the contractor, who has usually had nothing to do with the design process, examines the drawings and makes his bid. Industry supplies raw materials and components and has little contact with the contractor. The various building material manufacturers make their components totally independently of each other. They do not develop a product with an overall view of the complex it goes into. It is an absurd industry, inefficient in comparison with any other area of manufacturing. The design process is done over and over again; the architect has to invent the wheel every time. The contractor, on the other hand, cannot put his own experience into the design process; he gets a set of drawings as a *fait accompli*.
>
> From the time I started working on my thesis, I felt that the whole construction process had to be put into the factory, with all that implies. I studied what was considered in Europe to be industrialized housing. All their systems in 1959 and 1960 were based on panel construction. The walls, floors, and ceilings of a house were manufactured in a factory. The rest of the building was more or less conventionally finished. This seemed a limited system, since even if you could perform a miracle and produce the shell at no cost at all, all you were doing was cutting the construction cost by 25 percent because 75 percent of the house isn't in the shell.
>
> I concluded, any system that didn't permit you to take 75 percent into the factory was automatically obsolete. I

Safdie's modular Habitat complex in Montreal. The crane in the background lifts each unit into position (MOSHE SAFDIE & ASSOCIATES)

Another view of Habitat with its glass-enclosed walkway (MOSHE SAFDIE & ASSOCIATES)

also felt that the limits on these systems forced the architect to produce a vertically stacked cellular beehive of an apartment building. All the components met at corners, and corners are always the weakest point in the structure. Only in the USSR was there further experimentation: instead of prefabricating panels, they were prefabricating whole rooms.

So I came to the conclusion, as others have, that in order to take that 75 percent into the factory, you had to deal not with panels but with volumes of space. You had to prefabricate cells of space in the factory, and put your mechanical services, plumbing, bathrooms, whatever else there was, into them in an assembly-line procedure. You would then assemble the modules on site and, if connections were simple, you would have a 95 percent factory-produced building. This was the first very important implication of making houses in a factory."*

In terms of manufacturing, Safdie's view is exceptionally logical. So logical is it that the mobile and modular building industries have blossomed and quite clearly prove the economies inherent in manufactured housing to the consumer.

However, builders, be they of conventional homes or manufactured homes, seek the largest common denominator and, in so doing, sacrifice individuality to economy. There is nothing wrong with buying a home that looks like every other one on the street, providing it fits the site and that is what you want.

Safdie and others proved conclusively that modular structures need not be pedestrian. His design is unique and exciting; the designs most often offered individual buyers of modular homes are not.

In our experience, there is a curious chicken-and-egg syndrome among builders of all kinds. We have suggested to builder friends that they provide new, stick-built

* Moshe Safdie. *Beyond Habitat* (Cambridge, Mass.: MIT Press, 1970), pp. 111–112. Reprinted by permission.

homes with greater individuality and within a variety of modern styles. They'd like to, they say, but the public wants Cape Cods and kitsch colonials and aluminum-sided ranches. How can you say that, we counter caustically, when you offer the public no alternative? But the public clearly wants what we offer, say they, for it continues to buy our houses. One builder friend raised an even more basic question: Does the public know what it wants?

Finnish architect Aarno Ruusuvuori of Helsinki offers an alternative. It is a box, but what a box! Ruusuvuori capitalizes on the box-like shape and makes the shape even more interesting by using windows of different shapes and even using the geometrical design of a hot-water radiator as a visual element. The modular unit shown is a one-bedroom model, which is quite spacious. And the wooded setting makes it even more attractive. The architect calls it the Marihouse, for it was designed for Marimekko, Finland's internationally known fabric designer and manufacturer. Much interest in the project has been shown in Finland, the United States, and Japan, but at the moment it is not in production. Perhaps some day it will be available to Americans seeking a modular home with flair and taste. It is more attractive in our eyes than most modulars manufactured here.

Modular Homes

A modular home in the United States—often referred to as a "sectional" or "three-dimensional" home—generally consists of two rectangular units approximately 12′ wide and of equal length. An A-frame modular is also available. Mobile and modular home widths are the same because of the maximum width restrictions of highways. Even though the modular is delivered by truck, like a mobile home, once it is placed on its foundation it cannot be uprooted and moved elsewhere.

About 85% to 95% of work on the modular home is completed at the factory prior to shipping. A few on-site operations

Exterior of Ruusuvuori's Marihouse (AARNO RUUSUVUORI, ARCHITECT)

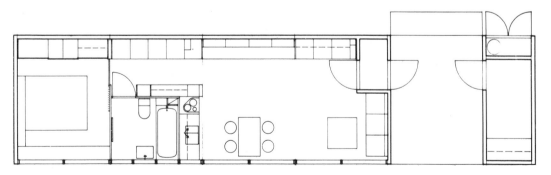

Marihouse floor plan (AARNO RUUSUVUORI, ARCHITECT)

Interior view of the Marihouse (AARNO RUUSUVUORI, ARCHITECT)

are necessary, such as providing the foundation and utility lines and services, attaching the modular to the foundation, some minor finishing work, and hookups.

The amount of work needed after the units are placed on the foundation is absolutely minimal; you could probably move in within a matter of hours after the units are delivered and attached. Therefore, it may be considerably easier for a modular or mobile manufacturer to give you a move-in date that he can keep.

Factory construction, in theory at least, has certain advantages for the modular or mobile home buyer. We seem to assume that conveyer belt assembly, under rigidly controlled conditions, will produce better quality control and a reasonably consistent product, while on-site stick-built construc-

tion quality may fluctuate with the quality of the work crew. We have seen ghastly factory-produced mobiles and modulars and equally ghastly stick-built homes.

Modular homes are in dead center of the industry in terms of quality and cost. They are competitive with double-wide mobiles and smaller prefabricated homes. The higher end of the mobile range is competitive with the lower-to-middle range of modulars, while the more expensive modulars are competitive with the less expensive prefabricated homes.

Some prefabricated home manufacturers claim that modulars are uneconomical because the modular maker is shipping boxes of air, whereas the prefabricated home manufacturer ships his materials tightly compressed, because they are not fully assembled. It seems a good argument, until you remember that the cost of transportation is very small when compared to total costs, and on-site labor, which is required to erect the prefabricated home, is a lot more expensive than the factory labor used by the modular industry.

Individual modular homes are usually built of wood, which though heavier than aluminum is lighter than other materials, an important factor in transportation. The industry generally considers a 300-mile radius from the factory to be the maximum transportable distance for a home. The mobile home industry uses the same figure. BurKin Homes, which manufactures the modular A-frame, will ship within a 1200-mile radius of their Michigan and Alaska plants, and they charge a lower cost-per-unit-per-mile rate than their competitors, perhaps to encourage distant buyers. The location of your building site will define those manufacturers whose products you can consider. (Use your road maps.)

The modular home industry, like that of mobile and prefabricated homes, is one of flux, with new companies coming into existence while others are leaving the field. Some modular manufacturers began as mobile home manufacturers, and others were builders of conventional stick-built housing. Each claims his previous experience is a virtue. The former mobile home people point to an expertise in factory production, while the former stick-built people claim a greater understanding of quality and craftsmanship.

Costs

There are a number of elements which contribute to the total cost of a modular home, and they appear in the checklist at the end of this chapter.

Two rectangular modular units in a factory (CONTINENTAL HOMES)

The dealer and manufacturer will provide firm costs for several items: cost of the unit you select, cost of transportation, and cost of installation and hook-ups. Just about everything else will be your responsibility. Your dealer, if he is local, may act as the contractor if you wish or, if not, should be able to steer you to the proper excavators and masons, electricians, and plumbers, and he may give you an estimated figure covering all costs beyond your payment to the manufacturer. Remember, however, that the dealer is anxious to make a sale, and if he thinks a low cost figure will clinch it, he may not hesitate to quote low.

As you know, costs fluctuate wildly these days. The prices mentioned in this book should be considered only as rule-of-thumb figures in establishing relationships between models and manufacturers. The only true costs are those quoted by the manufacturer or dealer.

As the size of a house increases, its overall cost increases, but its cost per square foot decreases. This inverse ratio occurs because the expensive utilities—major appliances, boiler, heating system, water heater, water pump, and so forth—are amortized over a larger area. This ratio applies to all forms of housing. Further, a two-story home will cost less than a one-story home given the same area because the two-story home would have a smaller foundation and roof and the two-story home would also have fewer linear feet of plumbing than an equivalent ranch home. The two-story home also is more economical to maintain and repair, and it may be cheaper to heat.

In 1972, modular homes were selling at $7.35 to $13.57 per square foot, with most units in the $9 to $12 range. The unit with the highest cost per square foot had only 700 square feet at a total package cost of $9,500. In 1974 manufacturers were loathe to quote prices; however, two manufacturers quoted $18 to $20 per square foot, which included transportation, installation, and finishing, while a third manufacturer quoted $14 to $16 per square foot without transportation, installation, and finishing.

A finished modular home (CONTINENTAL HOMES)

The variation within the price range is attributable to better-quality materials and options selected (like glass walls and large roof overhangs) as well as an understanding of precisely what is included in the base package price. For example, in some cases appliances were included, while other manufacturers omitted them in their quotations. Speaking broadly, the houses which we examined ranged in size from 20′ by 32′ (640 square feet) to 24′ by 70′ (1680 square feet), at an average, in 1972, of about $10 per square foot, or between $6,400 and $14,880.

Remember, if you plan to build a basement below a one-story modular home, you can increase the potential square footage of your home by 100%, less if you plan for less than a full basement.

The cost of the foundation will vary with size, complexity (problems with the land), and the availability of a labor force. One estimate that was current a few years ago was $950 for an 1100-square-foot foundation. Erection and finishing costs ranged, again several years ago, between $1,100 and $2,100. In some cases these costs fluctuated widely even with modular homes of the very same size. To further confuse you, costs fluctuate widely between different parts of the country; clearly, costs will be higher in wealthier parts of the country.

Transportation costs also vary. A few years ago manufacturers were quoting between $0.75 and $1.80 per mile per modular unit, or $1.50 to $3.60 per mile for the standard two-unit modular home. Prices also may vary with the length of the modular home. The range, it seems to us, is unreasonably wide.

Here's a rough rule of thumb: When a dealer quotes a manufacturer's price at the plant, add on an additional one-third to cover the foundation, erection, finishing, and hookups. This third does not include land, utilities, transportation, or any options which you select. Base price is what we're talking about for a modular unit of about 1,100 square feet.

Floor Plans

Most modulars are pure rectangles, without wings of any sort. Almost all modular homes are constructed from two units placed side by side, each of which usually has a width of 12′ and a maximum length of around 70′ (for 1680 square feet)), which can be doubled if the modular home is placed above a basement or lower floor. Two manufacturers, New England Modular Homes and Stylhomes, offer 28′-wide modular homes made up of two 14′-wide modules. At present, only 39 states permit 14′-wide modules to use their highways, and this is probably the single most important factor which has prevented the widespread use of 14′ units.

The most common width is 12′ per unit, though some "vacation home" modulars are available in two 10′ wide units. One manufacturer, Capital Industries, makes a 27′-wide line; the manufacturer sets two 12′-wide modules on a 27′-wide foundation and fills in the remaining three feet on the site. This additional width was expensive, adding close to $1,000 to the overall cost in 1972.

Modulars are generally "two rooms wide," with each room in the home not being more than 12′ wide unless it stretches the full width of the house, or 24′. In those floor plans that have corridors, the rooms along one side of the corridor have a maximum width of 9′, and on the other side, a maximum width of 12′.

One-bedroom modulars are rare, as are modular homes with more than four bedrooms. However, additional bedrooms can be supplied in a basement or lower floor. The average modular floor plan is two to four bedrooms, kitchen, living room, and a dining room, which in most cases is an L-shaped extension of the living room.

Two-bedroom modulars are generally 24′ wide and between 32′ and 44′ long. Three-bedroom modulars are generally 24′ wide and between 36′ and 52′ long; four-bedroom modulars are generally 24′ wide and 44′ to 70′ long. In area, two-bedroom modulars

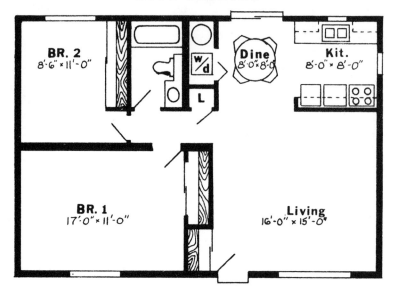

A standard two-bedroom floor plan; 24' x 36'

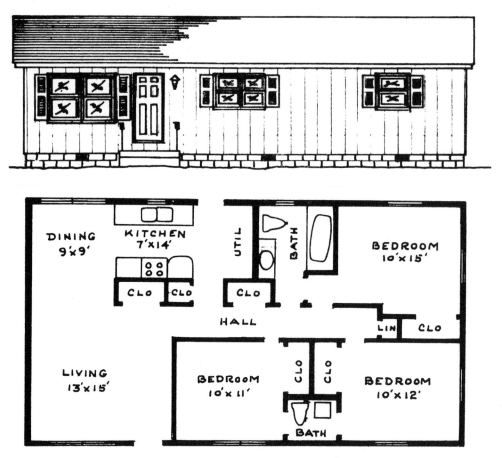

A standard three-bedroom floor plan and elevation drawing; 24' x 44'

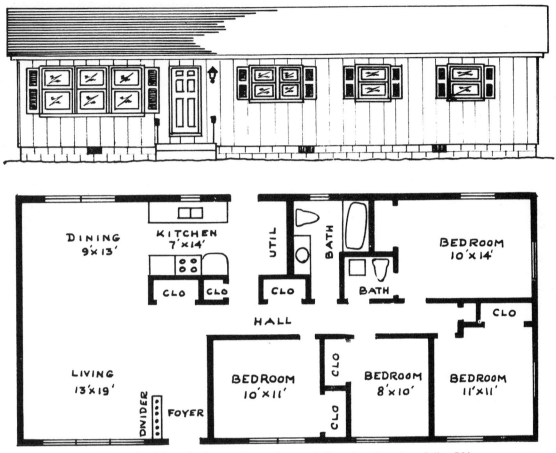

A standard four-bedroom floor plan and elevation drawing; 24' x 52'

range between 768 to 1056 square feet; three-bedroom modulars range between 864 and 1356 square feet; four-bedroom modulars range between 1056 and 1680 square feet (assuming no lower story).

Room sizes of modular homes, though larger than single-wide mobile homes and about the same size as double-wide mobile homes, are somewhat smaller than average rooms of stick-built and prefabricated homes.

The location and relationship of rooms in one-story modular houses is almost universal, with the bedrooms at one end of the house and the living room, kitchen, and dining area at the other. Space is efficiently organized, but the amount of storage space is not overly generous. This is by no means the fault of the manufacturers but is another result of the maximum widths allowed on highways. Perhaps a lower floor or basement, a

storage shed or garage would solve whatever storage problems you may have. With this in mind, a number of manufacturers indicate in their plans how the small space allocated for laundry equipment can be converted into a stairwell leading to a lower floor.

Furthermore, many manufacturers offer a bi-level line (also called a split foyer or raised ranch) which increases area as well as cost, for the upper level comes from the factory fully constructed, but the lower level is built and finished entirely on the site. Bi-levels have two stories, one of which is partially in the ground. Bi-levels are best built on sloping land so that one can enter the home from both levels. The lower level of a bi-level is in lieu of a basement.

As for two-story homes, New England Modulars offers several models with Dutch gambrel roofs. The first story follows the basic modular house plan and is received at

A garrison-style modular bi-level

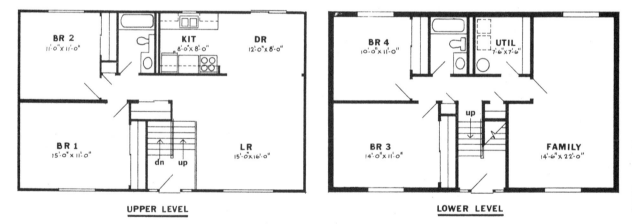

UPPER LEVEL

LOWER LEVEL

Floor plan for a modular bi-level: the upper level is made by the manufacturer as shown while the lower level plan is the manufacturer's suggested use of space

the site fully built. The second story can be purchased finished or unfinished (weight-bearing walls and windows only). The gambrel roofs are built on the site. These homes are "different" in appearance, and one would be hard pressed to identify them as modulars. This manufacturer also offers several two-story models with pitched roofs that arrive at the site fully constructed, requiring only that the lower floor be attached to the foundation and the upper floor stacked above it.

Minor variations on these basic themes are rare but can be found. However, remember that the product must be made within an economical distance of your building site.

Two manufacturers — Stylhomes and

Timely—offer models with the living room-kitchen-dining area in the center of the house and bedrooms on either side. This would appeal to those who wish to separate the sleeping and play quarters of children from adult quarters. Continental Homes has models with modules placed at right angles to one another rather than side by side. This allows each "zone" of the home greater privacy, makes the exterior more interesting, and creates useful sheltered outdoor spaces.

One especially interesting plan varied from the standard practice of lining up of the two rectangular modules side by side. This approach, by a company now out of business, offset the modules, thereby creating two usable outdoor areas in the process—one used for a carport, the other for a deck. Another manufacturer (Post-Coach, its Glen Manor model) offers a split level for a three-level house.

We encountered only one unusual modular line. This is BurKin Homes Corpora-tion's line of A-frames called "Cedar Chalets." They are true modulars—shipped in sections to the building site, where the units are lifted with a crane or rolled onto the prepared foundation. The other A-frames we came across were all prefab-ricated. Several models within the Cedar Chalet line are available: one single-wide model measuring 13′ by 36′ (468 square feet) and two double-wide models measur-ing 22′ by 36′ (792 square feet) and 22′ by 40′ (880 square feet). The square footage figures given here are for the ground floor area. Each model has a second floor, and additional space can be gained if a full base-ment is provided.

Two- and three-bedroom models are available, the largest of which, the 22′ by 40′, has about 1250 square feet in all, the size of a small conventional house.

The line gets its name from the A-frame roof which is covered with cedar shakes, and since the roof also forms the exterior walls,

A rendering of a two-story modular home with a gambrel roof (NEW ENGLAND MODULAR HOMES)

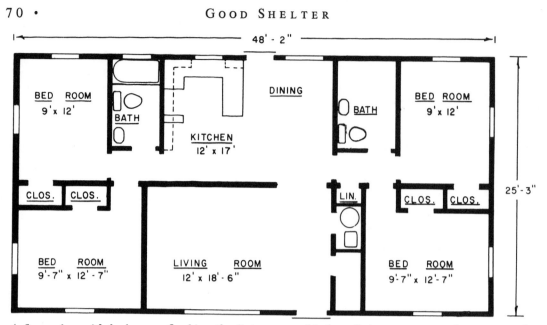

A floor plan with bedrooms flanking the living room-kitchen-dining room area (STYLHOMES)

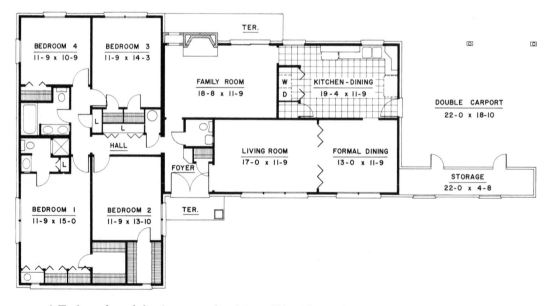

A T-shaped modular home made of four 12'-wide modules (CONTINENTAL HOMES)

this is the predominant feature of the house. The units come with lamps, drapes, carpeting, and appliances, and you can order optional furniture so that the home is ready almost immediately after it is placed on the foundation.

The manufacturer provides a one-year warranty. The cost, in 1974, was about $17.50 to $22 per square foot for the units themselves, not including foundation, hookups, transportation, and installation.

BurKin homes are manufactured in Michigan and Alaska and are sold within a 1,200-mile radius of their plants. At 1974 transportation costs of $1.30 to $1.50 per mile (this is a total figure for both modules), these homes are particularly attractive within a few hundred miles of the plant.

A modular A-frame (BURKIN HOMES CORP.)

What about floor plan changes of modular homes? Manufacturers can make some variations to accommodate the buyer. Needless to say, if only because the *raison d'être* of a modular home is factory construction, the scope of modifications is limited. In some cases, manufacturers will state unequivocally, in their brochures, that no variations on standard floor plans are available. Remember that whatever it is you would like to change would have to be accomplished within the basic 12′-wide structure mounted on a truck and would also have to sustain the stresses of transportation for substantial distances.

Some structural options (by no means radical changes) are available and are some-

times specified by manufacturers in their brochures. If they are not, ask the manufacturer or his dealer for a listing. Here are some of the common options offered at the time of writing: reversing the floor plan (for instance, if a cluster of bedrooms is on the right and you want them on the left); adding closet space (which reduces living area); shifting interior partitions to make a room larger (and the adjoining room smaller); or eliminating non-weight-bearing partitions entirely to make one large room of two small ones.

Although each house is constructed after the order is received, the plans are standard. Major variations require the manufacturer to draw special plans, may require additional

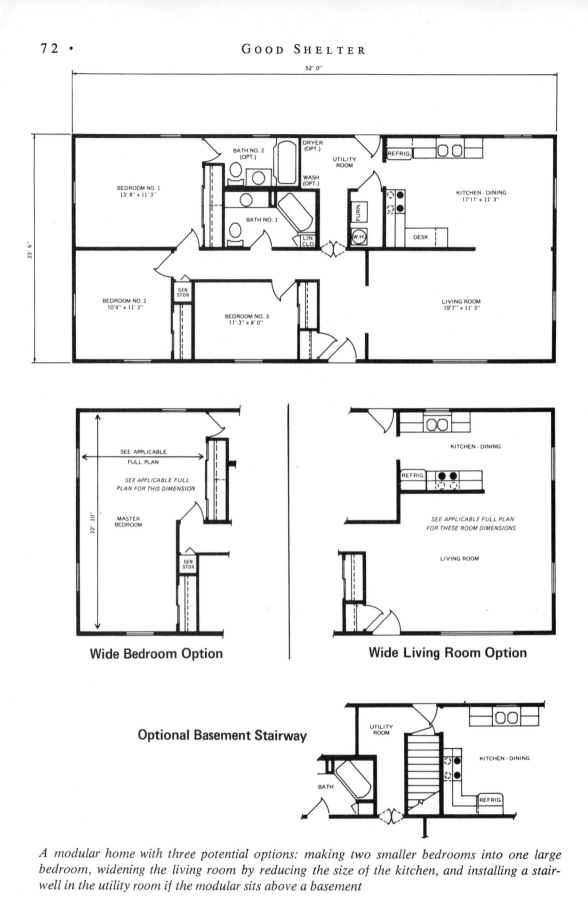

A modular home with three potential options: making two smaller bedrooms into one large bedroom, widening the living room by reducing the size of the kitchen, and installing a stairwell in the utility room if the modular sits above a basement

supervision in the factory, and, consequently, may require an additional fee. A few years ago one company asked for a fee of $250 for what it called a "major floor plan change," over and above whatever additional labor and materials were needed.

The main entrance of most modular homes opens directly into the living room, on the long side of the house, which may be a drawback to you. An alternative offered by several manufacturers is called a "narrow entry" model with the entrance on the narrow side of the house, either into the living room or into the kitchen.

One manufacturer, The Reasor Corporation, offers a "room-mate," an additional room which can be bought at a later date, if desired, and attached to the rear of the house. If you are interested in an option of this kind, we would advise that you check it out carefully at the outset. It may pay to extend the foundation of the modular in preparation for the eventual addition of a room. It is cheaper to have all foundation work done at the same time than to do it in shifts, and one continuous foundation is stronger than a foundation with an addition.

Exterior Design

Modular exteriors, like the floor plans themselves, are limited by the structure and size requirements. They are long and narrow, with low pitched roofs. Their siding, shutters (always fake), and roofing materials are of the grade used on many conventional homes. Unlike mobile homes, virtually all of which have metal siding and almost-flat roofs, and rarely have even fake shutters as standard equipment, modular homes are very close in materials, appearance, and construction to stick-built homes.

Most modular manufacturers offer a choice of exterior details, such as horizontal clapboard-like siding or vertical rough-sawn plywood, cedar shakes, window shutters of various lengths, special effects such as divided windows for the "colonial" look, bow windows, and steeper pitched roofs. The usual modular roof is 3:12 (in inches, the first figure is the vertical rise, the second the horizontal) or 2½:12 but one may purchase, for an additional fee, a 4:12 or 4½:12 roof. By contrast, the minimum pitch of a stick-built ranch house would be 5:12. Steeper pitched roofs are desirable for a number of reasons: less wind damage, longer life, lower maintenance, fewer leaks, better ventilation, and ability to shed snow. A-frames, whose roofs are very steeply pitched, are popular in heavy snow areas.

The illustrations on page 75 show the difference in appearance between the various roof lines.

Steeper pitched roofs cost more and last longer. They cost more because they must be specially built to fold down during transportation and are then erected after the modules have been set on their foundation.

Sun decks, glass walls, and overhanging roof gables are generally found in models called "vacation cottages" and would be appropriate for those who lead an outdoor-oriented life. There is no reason whatever to think of a "vacation cottage" as anything less than a year-round home if the structure is properly insulated and contains an adequate heating system. These homes do tend to be somewhat smaller in area than those called "year-round," but don't let the label turn you off if the living area is adequate for your needs. One manufacturer, Timely Corp., offers several of these "vacation cottage" features as options on all of its models.

The function of many of the options offered is to make the modular home resemble more closely conventionally built homes. Assuming you do not wish the exterior options but still would like the modular home to blend with a community of conventionally built homes, one approach would be to site the modular wisely and to landscape it well, a step we recommend highly and describe in greater detail on pages 41-44.

Several front exteriors offered by one manufacturer (ROYCRAFT INDUSTRIES-CONTEMPRI HOMES)

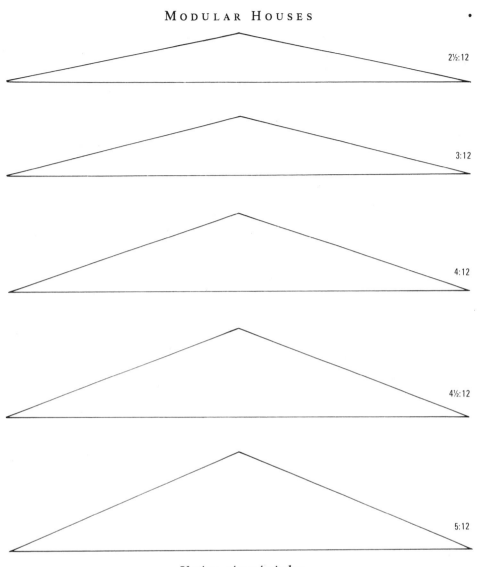

Variety of roof pitches

Interior Details and Furnishings

Inside, a modular home looks almost exactly like a conventionally built home. Modulars, unlike most mobile homes, come unfurnished, although a few manufacturers offer furnishing packages as options.

Walls and ceilings are generally wallboard or, less often, wood paneling. Manufacturers offering the paneling as standard often offer wallboard as an option. The floors are usually plywood or composition board subflooring with carpet or vinyl (called "roll goods") laid on top. In general, the mate-rials used in modular homes are similar to those used in conventionally built homes, but if there is any variance it is to a lower grade.

Some manufacturers offer two versions of their homes, standard and deluxe. Others offer a standard package of low-cost mate-rials with higher grade materials as options. Some of the options available are fancier than the standard items, and in some cases, the standard items are more attractive, being simpler in design. Here is an example of the differences between one manufacturer's standard and deluxe lines.

	Standard	*Deluxe*
walls	paneled throughout	wallboard with paneling
bathroom sink	standard sink	lavinette
floors	vinyl in kitchen, hall, bathrooms, and one bedroom; carpet in balance	oak floors except for vinyl in kitchen, and carpet in one bedroom; ceramic tile in bathroom
wall details	fabric accent wall in living room	fabric accent wall and molding in living room
other details	——	planter; full-length mirrors in bathroom

One manufacturer, Mod-u-Kraf Homes, offers decor-coordinated "theme" units, such as English Tudor or Swiss Alpine. The theme is carried out by a "mural wall" in the living room, an "accent wall" in the dining room, and coordinated bathroom mirrors, lighting fixtures, kitchen cabinets, and some exterior details, all of which are options and add to the cost.

As you go about investigating the lines of various manufacturers, check carefully on two details in particular—ceiling height and window size and placement. Ceilings in modular homes are generally 7½′ high, while conventionally built homes start at 8′ and go higher and mobiles are generally 7′ high. A particularly tall person might feel hemmed in by a low ceiling. Some manufacturers offer a cathedral ceiling in the living room, which might help. This ceiling follows the pitch of the roof and, as a result, the steeper the pitch, the higher the ceiling on the inside.

Windows tend to be small and are frequently placed high above the floor. On the one hand, this allows for more storage space and furniture placement along the walls; on the other hand, the location of these windows prevents you from looking outside if seated and it is difficult to escape through a high window in the event of a fire. Smaller windows also cut down on ventilation and natural light. It might be wise to find out whether the manufacturer offers options for lowering the windows or for larger windows. One company specifically lists such window options; others might comply, even though it is not a listed option.

Before and After the House Arrives

Preparation for the arrival of the units includes construction of a foundation and preparing the utility systems for an easy and efficient hookup when the units are in place.

A modular home must be placed on either a full basement, lower level, or crawl space, because all utility connections are beneath the floor and room for access is required. A modular home cannot be placed on a slab. If you are planning a crawl space, do not skimp; it should be adequate for plumbers and electricians to have room to work, not only for initial hookups but also for subsequent repairs. And don't forget to install a vapor barrier in the crawl space to reduce potential moisture problems.

Once the units are set and the hookups made, the site finishing or trim-out is done, including the installation of siding over the joint between the modules so that the siding is continuous, raising the roof if its pitch is steeper than road heights permit, patching any cracks caused by transportation, installing light fixtures, and any last-minute touch-ups that may be needed. There will also be exterior construction needed, such as installing entrance steps, carports and garages, and final grading and landscaping, but these may be done by the homeowner.

Time

The entire process, from signing of the contract with the manufacturer to moving-in date, can take anywhere from 6 to 12 weeks, assuming you don't run into any major weather or other difficulties in getting the foundation prepared and utility lines in. Once the modules arrive, the amount of delay is minimal. One manufacturer esti-

1. *Foundation and basement*   2. *Crane places first half of home onto the foundation*   3. *Crane lowers second half into place*   4. *Crane is removed*   5. *The house is ready for on-site finishing* (NEW ENGLAND MODULAR HOMES)

mates 64 man-hours (four men working eight hours a day for two days) are needed for the finishing touches once the house has been brought to the site. The estimate, however, does not include final grading and landscaping or any exterior construction. Here is the manufacturer's breakdown:

Operation	Time in Man-hours
Setting house on foundation	15
Roof assembly	20
Installing siding over joint	2
Interior assembly	8
Water and sewer connections	8
Electricity connections and exterior lights	8
Final clean-up	3
	64

The question of foundation should be given some thought. Some manufacturers will supervise foundation building; others may offer this service but only within a limited radius from their plants. In other cases, the manufacturer's representative or dealer may erect the foundation with his own crew or will subcontract the construction. The buyer may want to or have to act as his own subcontractor for the work. In any event, try to understand exactly who

UNIBUILT CONSTRUCTION   CONVENTIONAL CONSTRUCTION

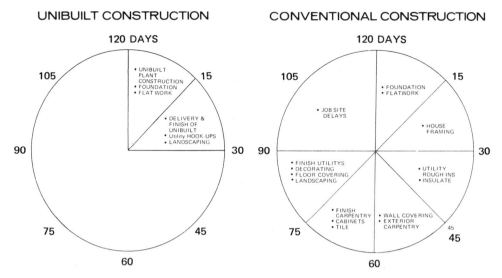

One manufacturer's comparison of time required to build a modular vs. conventional home (UNIBUILT STRUCTURES DIVISION OF THE REASOR CORP.)

does what concerning the foundation. Ask the manufacturer or dealer, and find out early in the game.

How to Buy and Finance a Modular Home

Some manufacturers require that their dealers maintain one or more models which prospective customers may inspect. There are also modular brokers who represent several manufacturers. In some cases, real estate brokers also sell modular homes.

Write to as many manufacturers as you wish, whose plants are located within a reasonable distance from your land. They will send you the names and addresses of their representatives and their descriptive literature. Be prepared to deal only with the representative, for few modular manufacturers deal directly with the consumer.

The advantage, in theory, of dealing with a franchised agent is that the agent should be thoroughly familiar with the manufacturer's product, knows how the foundation is to be prepared, how the modules are placed on the foundation, and so on. Some companies will, at a fee, provide on-site supervision for erecting and finishing the home.

Your bank will treat a modular home

like a conventionally built home, and you can get a mortgage like anyone else. You can also get a construction mortgage (see page 21) if you need it, if you qualify, and if mortgage money is available.

The manufacturer or dealer will specify his own payment schedule, perhaps requiring a deposit when the contracts are signed and the balance in a series of payments or in full upon final completion of work. Work done by a contractor or subcontractor hired by you will usually be paid upon the completion of that work, regardless of the manufacturer's schedule. You will be paying out varying sums of money throughout the building process, and that is why you might be interested in a construction mortgage. Don't be afraid to talk frankly with an officer of a lending institution. You will often find him a good source of information as well as a good source of money.

A word about warranties and guarantees. Read these documents carefully and ask your attorney to look them over line by line. It is important to know exactly who—manufacturer or dealer—is responsible for what. The last thing you want is to be embroiled in a running battle between the two, each accusing the other of causing whatever damage is in question. While the manufacturer and dealer hassle it out, the damage is not corrected and it is the buyer, as is always the case, who suffers. Responsibilities should be clearly stated in warranties and guarantees.

For your convenience, we've prepared the following chart listing those modular manufacturers who answered our inquiries.

Other companies are mentioned in industry lists available to the public (see Bibliography).

"Standard floor plans" refers to the basic floor plans described earlier.

AMERICAN MODULAR HOME CORPORATION (19 North Jensen Road, Vestal, New York 13850) has plants in New York, Arkansas, and Pennsylvania; minimum length 40', maximum length 48'; width 24'; options for fireplaces, cedar shakes, bow windows; standard floor plans.

ATLAS HOMES (249 Old River Road, Wilkes-Barre, Pennsylvania 18702) markets units in the northeast; minimum length 40', maximum length 48'; width 24'; standard floor plans.

BURKIN HOMES CORPORATION (White Pigeon, Michigan 49099) has plants in Michigan and Alaska; markets units within 1200 miles of its plants; minimum length 36', maximum length 40'; widths of 13' and 22'; A-frames only, called "Cedar Chalets."

CAPITAL INDUSTRIES (P.O. Box 326, Avis, Pennsylvania 17721) markets units within 350 miles and in 14 states; minimum length 42', maximum length 54'; width 24' and 27'; offers standard and deluxe lines; standard floor plans.

CONTINENTAL HOMES (P.O. Box 1800, Roanoke, Virginia 24008) markets units within 350 miles of its plants in Virginia, New Hampshire, and Missouri; minimum length 36', maximum length 50'; width 24'; manufactures large modulars using two, three, and four modules; vacation cottages; standard floor plans; also manufactures prefabricated homes.

CRAFTMARK HOMES (4595 Morgan Place, Liverpool, New York 13088) markets units in New York, Pennsylvania, New Jersey, and Massachusetts; minimum length 40', maximum length 48'; width 24'; standard floor plans; also manufactures prefabricated homes.

GLOBE INDUSTRIES (P.O. Box 188, Peru, Indiana 46970); minimum length 42', maximum length 54'; 24' wide; standard floor plans; a narrow-entry model is offered.

A kitchen in a modular just off the truck prior to on-site finishing (CONTINENTAL HOMES)

INDUSTRIAL LAMINATES CORP. (P.O. Box 6292, Austin, Texas 78702) markets units in Texas; minimum length 32', maximum length 46'; width 24'; standard floor plans; offers a one-room plus kitchen vacation cottage.

MOD-U-KRAF HOMES (P.O. Box 573, Rocky Mount, Virginia 24151) markets units in Virginia, North Carolina, and Maryland; minimum length 40', maximum length 52'; width 24'; also offers line of vacation homes with minimum length 28', maximum length 48', width 24'; decks offered as options for vacation homes.

NEW ENGLAND MODULAR HOMES (Biddeford Industrial Park, Biddeford, Maine 04005) markets units in New England and northeastern New York; minimum length 38', maximum length 52'; width 24' and 28'; offers standard floor plans; offers a variety of two-story homes with gambrel roof, garrison, and Colonial styles, some with upstairs unfinished.

POST-COACH, INC.–GLEN MANOR HOMES (Danville, Pennsylvania 17821); minimum length 38', maximum length 54'; width 24'; offers standard floor plans and a tri-level model.

THE REASOR CORPORATION (P.O. Box 460, Charleston, Illinois 61920) markets units primarily in Illinois; minimum length 44', maximum length 52'; width 24' with a 36'-wide model (3 12'-wide units); standard floor plans; offers a narrow-entry model and "room-mate"; also manufactures prefabricated homes.

ROYCRAFT INDUSTRIES-CONTEM-PRI HOMES (117 First Street, Chesaning, Michigan 48616) markets units in Michigan and Ohio; minimum length 44', maximum length 52'; width 24'; offers a two-family modular unit; standard floor plans; brochure indicates dealers have more floor plans than those shown.

STYLHOMES (800 South Broadway, Riverton, Wyoming 82501) markets units in Wyoming only; minimum length 32', maximum length 52'; width 24' and 25' 3"; offers models with bedrooms flanking living room-kitchen in addition to standard floor plans.

TIMELY CORP. (P.O. Box 18165, San Antonio, Texas 78218) markets units in Texas; minimum length 32', maximum length 44'; width 20' and 24'; standard floor plans and units with bedrooms flanking living room-kitchen.

UNITIZED SYSTEMS COMPANY (USCO) (P.O. Box 127, South Hill, Virginia 23970) markets units in Virginia and Maryland; minimum length 38', maximum length 52'; width 24'; standard floor plans.

Please bear in mind that the above listing is presented only as a guideline. Since the time it was compiled, manufacturers may have altered lengths, expanded or contracted their marketing area, opened new plants or closed plants, and may offer new floor plans and options.

Cost Checklist

The list which follows is here to help you calculate just what your costs will be and will help you to make valid comparisons between different manufacturers and models. We recommend that you make a copy of these pages and answer all questions for each and every model you are considering. Comparing all of the completed checklists should indicate, roughly, which manufacturer is offering the better price. The cost checklist should be used in conjunction with the materials checklist at the end of the specifications chapter.

1. The Building Lot

Land	$_____
Lawyer (including all contracts for land and home, searches, closing, and anticipated appearances before local boards)	$_____
Land survey (if recent survey unavailable from seller)	$_____
Title insurance (one-time expense)	$_____
Land transfer taxes, if any	$_____
Building permit application fee	$_____

Building permit $_____
Soil percolation test (if you are
    installing a septic system) $_____
Soil log (for septic systems) $_____
Engineered septic design $_____
Septic system permit $_____
Well permit (if you have to dig
    your own well) $_____

2. The Modular Home

Modular home basic package $_____
Floor plan modification(s) $_____
Options (itemize) _____
_____
_____ $_____
Transportation to site, installa-
    tion, and finishing $_____
Total payment due to modular
    home manufacturer or dealer $_____
Taxes, if any, on purchase price $_____
Other necessary buildings (ga-
    rage, carport, storage sheds,
    etc.) $_____
Other exterior construction
    (stairs, patio, deck, etc.) $_____

3. Site Work

Land clearing, if necessary, to
    receive the modular home $_____
Preliminary grading $_____
Foundation (excavation and
    construction) $_____
Road or driveway construction $_____
Road or driveway surface
    (stone, macadam) $_____
Installation of above-ground
    electric service $_____
    or
Installation of underground
    electric service $_____
If underground and you pay for
    the trench, how much? $_____
If a transformer is required and
    you pay for it, how much? $_____
If the transformer requires a
    pad and you pay for it, how
    much? $_____
Electrical hookup from service
    line to home $_____

Installation of above-ground
    telephone service $_____
    Will the telephone company
    allow you to install under-
    ground service in the same
    trench with underground
    electric service?
Telephone installation (equip-
    ment, receivers, service
    charge) $_____
Septic system built to prevailing
    specifications or better $_____
Plumbing and hookup from
    septic system to home $_____
    or
Plumbing and hookup from
    home to existing public
    sewerage lines $_____
Cased-in well dug to prevailing
    specifications or better and
    desired water pressure $_____
Plumbing and hookup from
    well to home $_____
    or
Plumbing and hookup from
    public water supply to home $_____
Final grading $_____
Inspections $_____
Occupancy permit $_____

4. Other Expenses

Homeowner's insurance policy
    on the home per year (usually
    required by the lending in-
    stitution) $_____
Budget for landscaping per
    year (lawn, trees, shrubs,
    etc.) $_____
Estimated annual property taxes $_____
Other annual municipal taxes $_____
Estimate your annual mainte-
    nance costs (painting, clean-
    ing, general repairs) $_____

5. Utilities

Estimate your monthly electric
    bill $_____
Estimate your monthly gas bill $_____

Estimate your monthly fuel (for heating) bill $_____

Estimate your monthly telephone bill $_____

Estimate your monthly garbage collection bill if not provided by the municipality $_____

Estimate your annual bill for the use of public sewerage lines $_____

Estimate your annual bill for the use of public water supply $_____

6. Money

How much money will you need? $_____

How much money do you have? $_____

How much of the cash you have in hand will you be applying as a down payment on the modular home? $_____

How large a mortgage will you need? $_____

For how many years (when they tell you the monthly payment you'll know how long a period you'll need)?

For lending institutions (commercial banks, savings banks, and savings and loan associations):

Will you need a conventional mortgage or a construction mortgage? At what interest rate? (% per year)   _____%

Is the interest rate "simple interest" or "add-on" interest? If "add-on" interest, what is the "true interest" rate? (% per year)   _____%

If the lending institution charges a fee for processing your application, how much? $_____

If the lending institution charges "points," how much will this cost? $_____

Are there any other one-time fees or charges levied by the institution and how much will they cost? $_____

Does the lending institution penalize you for the early repayment of the loan? If so, what is the penalty? $_____

Does the monthly payment to the lending institution include all municipal taxes?

What is the total amount of money you will pay for your loan (the number of installments multiplied by the monthly payment)? $_____

Of this amount, how much is interest and fees (deduct the principal borrowed from the total amount of money you pay the lending institution)? $_____

PREFABRICATED HOUSES

(DECK HOUSE, FRED ROLA)

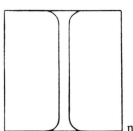n the housing industry, a prefabricated home is one built by a construction technique that involves the precutting and pre-assembly in a factory of some or all parts of a house. These elements are then shipped by truck to a building site for erection on a previously prepared foundation. When the package is unloaded, the manufacturer's obligation to the buyer is often concluded. When the on-site crew finishes its work, the buyer occupies the home.

Prefabricated homes have a poor reputation among some people. We came across an advertisement recently by a builder of on-site, stick-built homes who stressed that his product was "not a prefab." That does not strike us as something to brag about, given the many advantages of prefabrication.

A number of methods are included in the generic term "prefabricated"—"precut," "panelized," and "pre-engineered," all of which are used by the manufacturers themselves. Precut and pre-engineered are pretty much the same thing; panelized is a branch of the prefabricated housing industry which, instead of shipping precut pieces of lumber, sends fully factory-assembled panels to be erected on the foundation. Panelized assembly is faster than those forms of prefabricated housing where each piece of lumber must be attached to the next on the site. For the purpose of simplicity, we use the term "prefabricated" throughout this chapter.

Like the other forms of housing in this book, prefabricated homes have advantages and disadvantages.

Here are some of the advantages of prefabricated homes over mobile and modular homes.

1. *Cost.* The buyer can do some of the building work to cut costs, and he can do some or all of his erecting and interior finishing. The amount of work a mobile or modular owner can do is far more limited, except when a modular home is placed over a basement which will eventually be finished by the owner.

2. *Range of styles.* Prefabricated housing offers the widest range of home styles and materials.

3. *Site suitability.* Design can be readily varied to adapt the prefabricated home fully to its site.

4. *Floor plan flexibility.* A wide range of floor plans may be easily modified to suit virtually any life-style.

5. *Code conformity.* Construction techniques and materials, in many cases, may even exceed the requirements of local building codes, and where changes are required, they can readily be made.

(AMERICAN BARN)

6. *Delivery*. The prefabricated house package can be delivered to almost any site with a minimum of land clearing.

Prefabricated homes have some advantages over stick-built housing.

1. *On-site labor*. Prefabricated housing requires fewer on-site skilled labor man-hours.

2. *Materials cost*. Materials are purchased in vast quantities and are precision cut for optimal fit and minimum waste.

3. *Construction quality*. Quality control over materials is a result of factory production. This applies only to the package itself, for the quality of the erected home will depend on the quality of the on-site erecting and finishing crews.

4. *Construction time*. A prefabricated home will go up faster than a stick-built home. Panelized homes will go up faster than precut prefabricated homes. Modulars and mobiles go up virtually overnight.

Here are a few disadvantages of prefabricated housing.

1. *Cost*. Prefabricated homes cost more than mobiles and modulars because of the on-site labor and, at times, substantially better materials.

2. *On-site labor*. A crew may be difficult to hire in remote areas.

3. *Construction quality*. Subject to the quality of the on-site crew, which may range from excellent to horrid.

Buying and Building a Prefabricated Home

Building a prefabricated home presents some steps which are not factors for mobile or modular buyers, for prefabricated homes require piece-by-piece erection.

The quality of the builder of the prefabricated home is crucial to the success of the structure. In those instances where you hire a builder who does not represent the manufacturer, we strongly advise that you bring him into your planning well before your order for the home is placed.

Prefabricated homes are sold much like other forms of manufactured housing. Manufacturers advertise their products in newspapers and magazines and ask you to write for their catalogs. Because some of the catalogs are expensively printed, a small fee of a few dollars may be charged, but will be refunded if you order a home. Along with his catalogue a manufacturer might include a list of his dealers, agents, or representatives whom you can contact. It is a good idea to contact those who are closest to your building site.

The manufacturer's representative will meet with you and explain the product. He will visit the site to see if any site problems exist and often will suggest ways to site your home on the land.

Your contact should do much more than simply sell you a package. He should recommend qualified local builders if he himself is not a builder, and should be on hand to supervise construction of those elements for which he is responsible. Specify the hours and aspects of supervision on paper so that

(ACORN STRUCTURES, SAM ROBBINS)

the representative is obligated to put in his expertise and time.

Some manufacturers will supply you with lots of information but, when it comes to buying, will not sell to the consumer. They will sell directly to a builder of your choice, or their choice, and your contact and contract will be only with this builder. If you have any problems, the builder would be held responsible.

In general, if you are buying only the package, your contract with the manufacturer will cover only the quality of workmanship and materials of the package and insure that the materials were received in good condition. Herein is a potential problem, for the manufacturer does not and cannot vouch for the workmanship of the builder and, similarly, the builder does not vouch for the quality of materials received from the manufacturer. You might find yourself in a situation wherein the responsibility of making good is not clear. Two manufacturers specifically mentioned warranties on their materials: Acorn Structures for two years and Ivon Ford for 90 days. Warranties and guarantees on brand-name items are covered by their makers.

An authorized dealer, agent, or representative, if experienced, can be of great assistance as you redesign the manufacturer's plans to better suit your needs. (The same holds true for a franchised builder.)

This person, whose fee is included within your payment to the manufacturer, also should serve as your intermediary with the manufacturer, lending institutions, and the builder if he himself is not also the builder.

The on-site construction may be done by a recommended builder who has no official connection with the manufacturer or by a builder who may be franchised by the manufacturer. A franchised builder, ostensibly, is thoroughly familiar with the building system and its components; his estimates may also be substantially higher than those of a local builder). The franchised builder may quote a higher fee because he knows that the buyer will assume that he, the builder, will produce a better home than someone local with no specific prefabricated home building experience.

If your builder has no such experience, both you and your representative must stress as emphatically as possible that the builder read the erection manual and all other instructions provided by the manufacturer. This is not quite as simple as it seems. How many times have you bought a toy or other item that requires assembly and found yourself skipping from Step 6 to Step 9 because everything between seemed unnecessary? You usually are in such a situation on Christmas Eve, and after all of the shortcuts have been taken, the assembled item doesn't look right or starts falling apart. Imagine the potential problems of building a house from a manual if you don't do it properly from the start.

Some manufacturers may also serve as the contractor or builder of the home you buy, but usually only if your building site falls within a specified radius of the fabricating plant. This is the best possible way to build a prefabricated home, but it may also be the most expensive. If you are lucky enough to have this option, you might consider having the manufacturer's crew do most of the work, and either you or a local craftsman can finish the interiors.

Speaking very generally, the representatives of prefabricated housing whom we have met are more sophisticated than those who sell other types of housing. The polish does not make them any more or less trustworthy, and we advise that you check the credentials and track record of both the manufacturer and his representative.

After you have chosen the home you hope to build, and have met with the agent or representative of the manufacturer, find out exactly which parts of the house the manufacturer produces, where the rest of the house comes from, and just who does the on-site construction work. If the manufacturer does not sell a complete package, you or your builder may have to purchase additional materials for your home.

Some manufacturers supply a materials package that may include anything from ex-

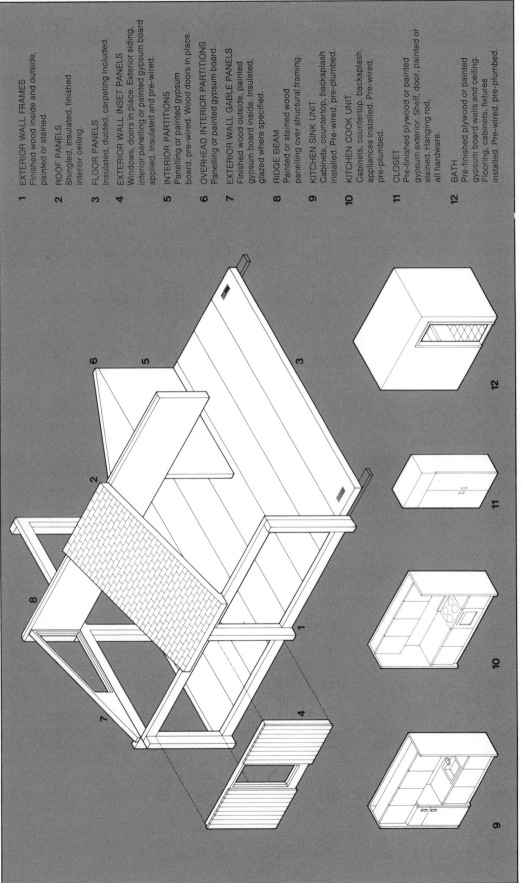

1 EXTERIOR WALL FRAMES
Finished wood inside and outside, painted or stained.

2 ROOF PANELS
Shingled, insulated, finished interior ceiling.

3 FLOOR PANELS
Insulated, ducted, carpeting included.

4 EXTERIOR WALL INSET PANELS
Windows, doors in place. Exterior siding, interior panelling or painted gypsum board applied. Insulated and pre-wired.

5 INTERIOR PARTITIONS
Panelling or painted gypsum board, pre-wired. Wood doors in place.

6 OVERHEAD INTERIOR PARTITIONS
Panelling or painted gypsum board.

7 EXTERIOR WALL GABLE PANELS
Finished wood outside, painted gypsum board inside. Insulated, glazed where specified.

8 RIDGE BEAM
Painted or stained wood panelling over structural framing.

9 KITCHEN SINK UNIT
Cabinets, countertop, backsplash installed. Pre-wired, pre-plumbed.

10 KITCHEN COOK UNIT
Cabinets, countertop, backsplash, appliances installed. Pre-wired, pre-plumbed.

11 CLOSET
Pre-finished plywood or painted gypsum exterior. Shelf, door, painted or stained. Hanging rod, all hardware.

12 BATH
Pre-finished plywood or painted gypsum board walls and ceiling. Flooring, cabinets, fixtures installed. Pre-wired, pre-plumbed.

A total system (OMEGA STRUCTURES; DAN KISTLER, AIA)

terior walls, doors, and windows only to all of the materials needed for a completed home (excluding foundation and other masonry). Whatever the manufacturer does not supply is purchased by the customer or his builder.

The most common prefabricated home package includes only materials for the shell of the house—floor framing and subfloor, exterior walls with windows and doors, roof framing and roofing, and interior partition framing. These elements may come in precut pieces or pre-assembled panels. Only two companies, Omega and Flexi-Panel, offer total systems including, for example, pre-installed wiring and heating units in wall panels or a "wet core" unit containing kitchen, bathroom, all plumbing lines, furnace, hot water heating, and electric box. One disadvantage of a "wet core" pre-engineered and pre-assembled system is that a number of large structural units make up the whole and special equipment, such as a crane, may be needed to set the "wet core" into place. On the other hand, a "wet core" would save the time and expense of skilled labor doing the plumbing and electrical work on the site from scratch. In the long run, you would probably save money by having a system which includes a "wet core." Such a pre-assembled unit would also benefit from the quality control available at the factory.

The manufacturer's package often excludes items such as insulation, wallboard, finish flooring, mechanical systems, appliances, and fixtures. Sometimes these items are offered as options, but since they are fairly standard items no matter what the style of the house, you can just as easily buy them locally. Many of these items are sold with guarantees and warranties, and it might be convenient to have a local dealer to whom you can take your problems and from whom you can expect service. It makes little sense to buy all of these elements from the housing manufacturer unless they come in pre-assembled units like "wet cores" or "plumbing walls." After all, the manufacturer buys them from someone else who in turn buys them from the maker; then the

housing manufacturer transports these same items to the customer's site.

In a few instances, manufacturers will offer extremely complete specifications lists which recommend materials and quality levels even for those elements not supplied by them. This is meant to assure an overall level of quality.

Because most of the construction takes place on the site and because most manufacturers provide materials for only a portion of the construction, it is usually possible to buy a prefabricated home at a stage which best suits your budget and your willingness and ability to do some of the work yourself. Here are the main forms:

Architectural materials package or kit. This is sold either to the builder or directly to the homeowner. It consists of one or more truckloads of materials delivered to the building site and may include some or all of the following: exterior walls, floor, roof, partition wall framing, doors, windows, insulation, stairs, interior trim, kitchen cabinets, and all hardware needed to erect the shell.

Full materials package or kit. This, too, may be sold directly to the builder or consumer. It consists of the architectural materials described above plus some or all of the materials to complete the house, such as plumbing, heating, electrical system, fixtures, appliances, wall finish materials, and finish flooring.

Erected shell stage. This is usually erected by the manufacturer for the buyer's local builder to finish, or it may be erected by the local dealer or builder for the buyer to finish. The shell is a weathertight structure on a foundation with all of the basic carpentry completed. It includes unfinished flooring, exterior walls, roof, and sometimes insulation and partition wall framing. It may or may not include delivery of a supplementary package with all of the remaining materials to complete the structure.

The erected shell stage is a good place to start if you plan to do a lot of the finish work yourself. One manufacturer, Ridge Homes, specializes in erecting shells and offers a full-color, 86-page magazine which discusses various do-it-yourself projects.

A note of caution: Descriptions of how to do your own plumbing, electric wiring, and such tend to sound much simpler and less time consuming than they actually are. Furthermore, it is imperative that you find out whether your local building code allows you to do any part of the work yourself. In many parts of the country, especially urban areas or areas where union labor is powerful, you may be required to have a licensed craftsman or union member do certain work, and an occupancy permit may be denied until you get a proper signature on a document. What would you do if, for an example of paranoia, the plumber or electrician refuses to certify your work and claims that what you have done is unacceptable? Read your building code carefully and find out what do-it-yourself work is permitted.

Rough finish stage. This is one step closer to a finished building than the erected shell stage. It is erected by a builder (sometimes, though rarely, by a manufacturer) for a less skilled or less ambitious do-it-yourselfer to finish. The rough finish stage includes everything you absolutely need to move in and finish the house bit by bit, as time permits. All of the elements listed in the erected shell stage are included, plus installation of all mechanical systems, insulation, and often sheetrock and other wall finish material. Among the chores left for you are finish flooring, kitchen cabinetry, interior trim, painting, and possibly even installing interior finished walls.

Turnkey-ready stage. All you have to do here is supervise the supervisors of the workers, make snap decisions in the event of an emergency, pray that you live to see the completed home, pay all of the bills if you do, and appear on a given day, put the key in the door lock, turn it, and move in.

These several stages allow for a maximum latitude to suit just about each potential home buyer. One can do as little or as much as one wishes, based on ability, time, and finances. Unless you are absolutely sure of your skills, we suggest that you speak with other do-it-yourselfers—amateur plumbers, electricians, carpenters, and masons—before you take the plunge.

Options

Options within the prefabricated home industry are varied, far more so than those available from other forms of manufactured housing. Because prefabricated houses are not subject to the rigidities inherent in assembly-line construction, there are many different styles and designs available. In a strict sense, everything not included within the manufacturer's package is an option.

Some manufacturers will sell, as options, some or all of the elements needed to complete the home beyond the exterior shell stage. As with all options, regardless of the type of home you buy, you must decide whether it is more economical to purchase the element from the manufacturer or to buy it locally.

More commonly, a manufacturer's options will be related to the architectural design of the house. You may have a choice of different sidings, doors and windows, or structural additions such as ells, carports, garages, porches, roofs of several pitches, overhangs, dormers, and other items. An option may be a substitution of equal or dissimilar items at the same or additional cost.

Some options offered are really extras that make your home fancier (such as vanities or sunken bathtubs), or that reduce future maintenance (for example, cedar or redwood siding). Other options might be considered assets (gutters, downspouts, greater insulation, etc.). When you go about comparing prices given by different companies, be sure the total prices include all of the options you require.

As with manufacturers of mobile and modular homes, some prefabricated home manufacturers have special features which are standard in their more expensive homes but are options in their smaller models. Bathroom vanities, fake ceiling beams,

Three exterior treatments of the same house (FLEXI-PANEL)

lighted ceilings, and mirrors are offered by one company in this way.

The manufacturer's specifications list will usually mention some of the more popular options. A complete options list, with detailed descriptions and costs, is usually available from the manufacturer or his representative, and you should study it carefully before you get down to the brass tacks of figuring out just how your home will look.

Time

How long does it take to build a prefabricated home? Estimates from manufacturers vary from one to six months from the signing of the contract to occupancy—a wide spread indeed. Assuming there are no unforeseen delays caused by bad weather or shortages of materials or labor, a more reasonable estimate might be between three to four months if all the work is done by hired, professional help. A stick-built home of about 1300 square feet constructed by a three-man crew should take five to six months from ground breaking to occupancy.

You could expect delivery of the package within one to two months following your signing of the contract, somewhat longer if you order the package at the height of the building season. The foundation should be prepared during this waiting period. Erecting the weathertight shell can take anywhere between one day to two weeks, depending upon the amount of pre-assembly of the components at the factory. Interior finishing and installation of the mechanical systems may take as much as several months to complete, again depending on the amount of factory or on-site assembly.

Prefabricated Housing Costs

Prefabricated homes are the cream of the manufactured housing industry, and they cost more than mobile or modular homes. The price range is as wide as the variety of styles, materials, and designs. Costs may be as much as for stick-built homes. Bear in mind architect Moshe Safdie's earlier remark that about one-quarter of the cost of the structure is for the shell, which is all that many prefabricated housing manufacturers provide. Some savings on mechanical systems would come from factory pre-assembled units, like "wet cores." If you do some of the finishing work or other steps yourself, you can potentially save more.

Completed prefabricated homes (not including land, on-site utilities, landscaping, and other site work) ranged from $14 to $29 per square foot in 1972 and $15 to $34 in 1974. Stick-built housing in the area in which we live was quoted at between $25 and $35 per square foot for a standard model home in 1974. In our opinion, some of the prefabricated manufacturers offer better designs, better, certainly, than some stock homes knocked out by local builders. The prices quoted above are for turnkey-ready homes; any work that you might do would lower the costs both of prefabricated homes and stick-built homes. Given the same quality of materials and construction, the smaller the house the higher the per-square-foot cost.

In 1972 we found a low of $10,500, and in 1974 a low of $21,000. The houses were somewhat different, with the highs in both years going well above $100,000.

Most manufacturers supply price lists; some will quote only on complete packages, while others will offer separate quotations on each stage of completion. The only price which can be quoted firmly by the manufacturer is the package cost, which is based on the quality of materials, uniqueness of design, size of the house (square feet), and floor plan.

Local labor costs fluctuate widely. One company has found the spread to be between $3 and $15 per hour. In general, when a manufacturer estimates cost of construction, he is thinking of a home built in an "average" suburban community which is neither high- nor low-income. The more expensive the cost of living in the area in which you intend to build, the higher your building costs, and the converse is true. However, costs may also be quite high in less expensive communities if skilled labor is not available locally and must be imported from other areas. This may be especially true in remote rural areas.

Anything that differs from the norm tends to cost more. Calculating costs and gathering estimates reminds us of a dialogue in the second act of DuBose Heyward's *Porgy and Bess:* Lawyer Frazier offers to sell Bess a divorce from Crown for "One dollar, dat is, if there ain' no complications." A voice is heard from the rear, "Dat gal ain' never marry!" and Lawyer Frazier says, "Ah, dat's a complication . . . but it take expert to divorce a woman what ain't marry, an' it cos' you, ahem, dollar an' a half," which Porgy proceeds to pay.

If no construction labor costs are estimated by the manufacturer, you might consider this rough rule of thumb: consider the package as one-half to one-third the cost of the finished home, depending on how inclusive the package is.

Comparing two different homes is a difficult matter, as you must be sure that you are comparing the same things. The only reasonable approach is to choose two or more homes that are roughly equivalent and get estimates, including any design changes you have in mind. These estimates should include costs of foundation and other masonry. The cost checklist at the end of this chapter and the checklist following the specifications chapter should be of some assistance.

A word here about transportation. Don't assume that a manufacturer farther away from your site will charge more to transport the package, though this would seem logical. Rates per mile vary. Some prefabricated home manufacturers use transportation as a selling point. Shipping mobile or modular homes, they say, is really shipping a big box filled with air, whereas shipping a prefabricated home is far more economical because the materials are tightly packed. This is all quite true; however, the cost of transportation is a small part of the cost of the home.

Although the manufacturer has the obligation to deliver the materials to the buyer (or builder), the receiver has the obligation to remove the materials within a specified period of time. The manufacturer will not allow the receiver to get the shipment, say, on a Monday and unload it at his, the receiver's, convenience. The manufacturer, or the manufacturer's trucker, wants the truck back.

The buyer, therefore, must have a crew ready to unload the shipment on a given day and given time. If the truck does not appear, the unloading crew must still be paid. Manufacturers do not take responsibilities for delays caused by natural events, such as floods or snow. This policy applies to almost all manufacturers of housing.

Floor Plans

Prefabricated homes offer the widest variety of floor plans in the manufactured housing industry, because of the inherent flexibility of the building methods. They do not have the width and length limitations of mobile and modular homes. Many prefabricated homes are built according to construction methods that permit virtually any arrangement of the interior space, because the interior walls used to delineate rooms do not support the roof structure and consequently can be placed wherever you choose. Prefabricated houses can be built as long, as wide, with as many stories and wings as your site, budget, and preferences will permit. In the case of panelized prefabricated homes, the lengths and widths will be de-

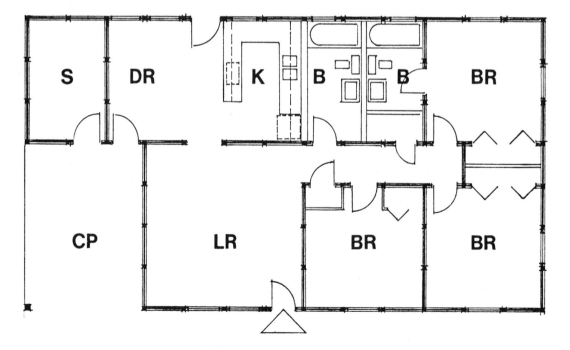

A floor plan divided into 4′ sections (FLEXI-PANEL)

A prowed vacation home with floor plan (HABITAT)

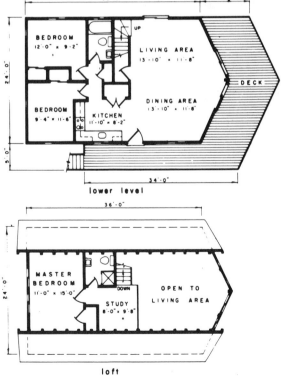

lower level

loft

termined by the size of the manufacturer's panels (usually in widths of four feet).

The number of floor plans offered by a given manufacturer can range from a few to hundreds. One company, Bow House, which sells a very specialized architectural product, has three basic plans. The largest companies that sell nationwide, Lindal Homes and National Homes, have 70 to 80 different plans in their catalogues. Several companies indicate that the plans shown in their literature are just samples of the "hundreds" that they or their dealers have on file. If you don't see exactly what you want, ask for it. Chances are excellent that you can get it.

Most manufacturers encourage the modification of their plans and have standard procedures for doing so. For example, Lindal Homes charges $25 for changes that only require modification of existing blueprints, such as moving a window, door, wall, or even switching rooms around. For major changes, for which new blueprints must be made, they charge $0.13 per square foot of the home's floor area, and then you will have to pay for whatever additional materials and labor may be needed. All manufacturers have architectural and drafting facilities for the preparation of "custom" plans.

You have undoubtedly come across the word "custom" in the literature of local builders and housing manufacturers. The word implies a structure in which every detail and element has been selected by the buyer. In fact, "custom" or "customizing" simply means that a builder or manufacturer can make some changes in the basic structure. Prefabricated housing manufacturers can make more and greater changes than any other manufactured housing maker, but you have to know your modifications or custom features *before* you order your package. Do not order a home that measures 28′ by 40′, and after the package arrives decide that you really want a 29′ by 52½′ home. Manufacturers will be reasonable if you will be, and a point is reached beyond which you cannot change your mind.

We have described the criteria for selecting a floor plan in the introduction and suggest that you go through the checklist at the end of that chapter as you look at the tempting, beautifully illustrated brochures.

Many manufacturers offer two or more housing lines, one for year-round living and another for "vacation" or "leisure" use. Year-round homes tend to be larger and more fully equipped than vacation homes, but as modifications are easy, you might consider modifying a vacation home for year-round living. Some manufacturers specialize in vacation homes.

Vacation homes tend to have more glass and more natural woods, decks, and balconies as well as smaller rooms, less closet space, and fewer square feet of living area. Some year-round housing manufacturers offer models with all of these design elements in their larger homes, plus greater living area and storage space.

There are four basic floor plan types: ranch, two-story, bi-level, and split level. Modular manufacturers make all of these types, too. But most modulars are ranches or bi-levels. Traditional-style homes follow these types closely, while modern homes diverge somewhat from the norm, but even an exotic-looking house will still function as one of these basic plans. The two domes in which we live are basically a ranch plan with an attic.

Most prefabricated home manufacturers offer plans in series, each floor plan being a variation in size or room arrangement on the basic plan of the series. A ranch series, for example, may have a dozen or so models ranging in size from 800 to 2500 square feet, all of which will derive from the same basic plan. The manufacturer may not call these homes "ranches" but may assign his own name to the series, such as The Millard Fillmore or The Shaker Heights.

The size range is defined by the manufacturer's intended market. Deck House, for example, offers homes ranging from 1500 to over 4000 square feet, while Ridge Homes stresses housing from under 1000 square feet to about 2600 square feet for families

A ranch with a provincial exterior (CONTINENTAL HOMES)

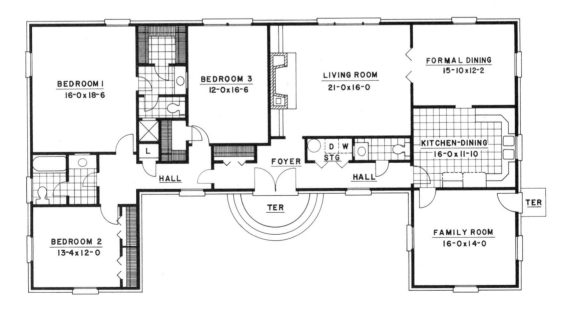

BEDROOM I
16-0 x 18-6

BEDROOM 3
12-0 x 16-6

LIVING ROOM
21-0 x 16-0

FORMAL DINING
15-10 x 12-2

L

HALL

FOYER

D W
STG

HALL

KITCHEN-DINING
16-0 x 11-10

TER

TER

BEDROOM 2
13-4 x 12-0

FAMILY ROOM
16-0 x 14-0

Floor plan for the provincial exterior ranch (CONTINENTAL HOMES)

who would like to do some of the work themselves.

Ranches. This is a broad term covering homes of one-story above the ground. Ranches may be built on a slab, crawl space, or full or partial basement. They are usually longer than they are wide. Most companies offer more ranch models than other plan types, and they may range in size from 600 square feet to over 3000 square feet. Small ranch homes of, say, two bedrooms and a living room-kitchen area may be called "cottages" in promotional literature.

Variations on the pure rectangle ranch include L- and T-shaped models—rectangles with wings. Ranch houses tend to cost more per square foot of area than two-story homes of equal size. Ranches tend to look best on flat, open land where their long, low shape hugs the ground. This sleekness may be emphasized by using horizontal siding and windows. Ranches are the only suitable form of housing for families having one or more members who are unable to climb stairs.

Bi-levels. This is a two-story home usually built on sloping ground so that one can enter the building from two levels. The front entrance is usually midway between the upper and lower levels. When you enter a bi-level you face stairs, a few steps up will take you to the upper level and a few steps down to the lower level. Sometimes called "split-foyer," "split-ranch," or "raised ranch," the bi-level usually has the living room, kitchen, dining area, and two or more bedrooms on the upper level, with additional bedrooms, family room, laundry room, and storage area or even garage on the lower level. The lower level is built partially into the ground and is in lieu of a basement.

Since the upper level is a self-contained house, the advantage of a bi-level for a family on a budget is that they can live up-

A bi-level, rear view (DECK HOUSE, FRED ROLA)

A two-story prefabricated home (NATIONAL HOMES)

stairs comfortably while they finish the lower level at their convenience. And the bi-level is one of the most inexpensive types to build because the foundation walls also serve as the walls for the lower story.

The typical floor plan of a bi-level has the advantage of any two-story structure having bedrooms on both levels: a family can "zone" the house with the parents upstairs and everybody else (children, in-laws, guests) downstairs. The bi-level's privacy arrangement is a clear plus. On the debit side, however, is having the kitchen upstairs while children who may need supervision are carrying on downstairs. Having a garage on the lower level requires one to carry groceries and other packages up a full flight of stairs. The lower level also may be prone to dampness if improperly constructed since part of it is built into the slope of the land.

Two-story. This structure has two full stories above the ground. It may be set on a full or partial basement, crawl space, or slab. It is sometimes called a "colonial," or with columns and a projecting roof it may be dubbed "Southern plantation style." You enter the home from the first story, which is at ground level. Full flights of stairs lead to the second floor and basement.

The most common floor plan calls for living quarters—living room, dining room, kitchen, and family room—at ground level and all bedrooms upstairs. In a typical plan, one enters through the main entrance and comes upon a central hall with a staircase leading upstairs. The first floor central hall opens to the rooms on the floor. Bedrooms and bathrooms open off the central hall on the second floor.

This floor plan offers good visual and sound privacy, for the sleeping quarters are removed from the part of the house in which adults will be spending evening hours and receiving guests. A very large two-story home might have the master bedroom on the ground floor, allowing even more separation between parents and everyone else.

A two-story home is economical and looks best on flat, wooded land. It costs more than a bi-level and less than a ranch, assuming each type has the same square footage. It is a vertical structure, and tends to loom up on flat, open land.

Some vacation versions of two-story

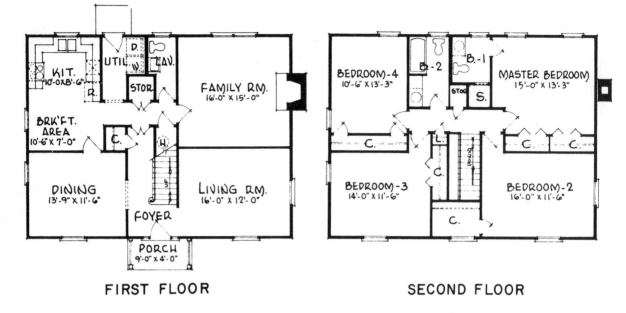

FIRST FLOOR   SECOND FLOOR

A floor plan for a standard two-story prefabricated home (MILLER MANUFACTURING CO.)

homes have living room, kitchen, and dining area on the upper story to take advantage of a better view from a higher elevation. Upper-story living rooms allow the owner to have a deck extending from the living room. A cathedral ceiling in an upper story living room, if the roof system permits it, can provide an open, spacious feeling.

In still another variation of the two-story vacation home, the living room is on the ground floor but is open to the upper ceiling. The second floor, with sleeping quarters, is like a loft and may be entirely open or divided into small bedrooms.

Other variations of the two-story home are the garrison, Cape Cod, salt box, and gambrel roof.

Garrison. In this style, the second floor is larger than the first and projects over it. In the garrison home, you would have a smaller foundation but a larger roof. The overhang from the projecting second story provides for natural protection for patios. Bi-level homes may also be built in this style.

Cape Cod. This two-story home has vertical walls for the ground floor only. The walls for the second story are formed by the roof and are, consequently, sloped steeply.

As a result, the amount of headroom upstairs is reduced and the space under the outer edges is useful only for storage. It is less expensive than a standard two-story home, because it eliminates the entire course of wall along the upper story. Cape Cods usually have windows on the second story only at the ends of the home (the structure's width); however, dormers can be set into the roof for additional natural light and more headroom, at somewhat higher cost.

Saltbox. This is a home with a very modern look despite the fact that it is 300 years old. It has a two-story vertical wall on one length and a one-story wall on the other. The peaked roof is of standard pitch on one side but extremely steep on the other. The long slope faced into winter winds can save you money on your heating bills.

Gambrel roof. Like the Cape Cod, the gambrel roof also· forms the walls of the upper story. Whereas the Cape Cod's roof is two flat planes meeting at the peak, the gambrel roof is curved, allowing for more headroom. The gambrel roof can also have dormers for windows at additional cost.

Split level. This style is sometimes called a "tri-level," for it has three levels arranged

A Cape Cod with bowed roof (top) *and its floor plan* (bottom) (BOW HOUSE)

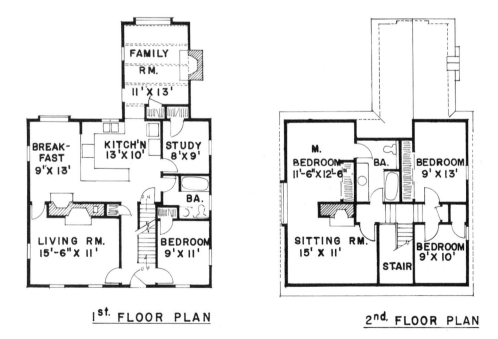

1st. FLOOR PLAN

2nd. FLOOR PLAN

A bi-level saltbox (ACORN STRUCTURES, SAM ROBBINS)

A log cabin with gambrel roof (VERMONT LOG BUILDINGS)

in two wings—a one-story wing attached to a two-story wing. The two-story wing is usually built partially in the ground, like a bi-level, and may also be built in garrison style.

One enters the home through the one-story wing which is at ground level and has the living room, dining area, and kitchen. Upstairs are the bedrooms; downstairs are the family room and utilities area (furnace, water heater, laundry, storage). The lower level may also include a garage.

Like the bi-level, the split level is best suited for a sloping site. A split level on a flat site would require much more grading than usual and might look awkward.

Split levels offer three separate activities areas—a reasonably private sleeping quarter, a separate area for children playing in the family room, and a portion of the home set aside for entertaining. To use this separation to best advantage, we suggest that your floor plans be drawn so that the stairs lead-

ing to the sleeping quarters or the family room not take traffic through the living room. Split levels also tend to have quite a bit of floor space.

Split levels are likely to require less stair climbing than two-story homes or bi-levels. As with the bi-level, the lower level of the split level can be left unfinished until you have the time and money to work on it. A portion of a split level is often partially in the ground and may have a tendency towards dampness if it is poorly constructed.

Manufacturers

Here are the 28 prefabricated housing manufacturers who responded to our requests for information. We have included descriptions of their marketing areas, the styles of houses they sell, construction techniques, and floor plans. "Traditional design" used below indicates a "colonial" look—

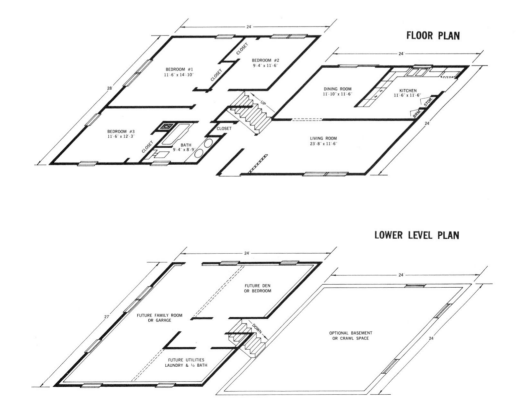

An especially easy to read split-level floor plan (IVON R. FORD)

clapboard siding (usually simulated), double-hung windows with shutters (usually fake), gable roof, etc. However, some manufacturers whose products are described as "traditional" offer options for streamlined variations of the traditional for a more contemporary look. "Standard floor plans" means ranches, bi-levels, two-story homes, and split levels with or without minor variations. We have characterized the sizes available in five categories: small—under 1000 square feet; medium—1000 to 2000 square feet; moderately large—2000 to 2500 square feet; large—2500 to 3000 square feet; and very large—in excess of 3000 square feet.

Other companies are mentioned in industry lists available to the public (see the bibliography).

ACORN STRUCTURES (Box 250, Concord, Massachusetts 01742). Sold throughout northeastern United States; large, established company with a good variety of styles. They specialize in simple, post-and-beam (described in the specifications chapter), contemporary designs of understated elegance marked by excellent planning and fine materials. Year-round and vacation home lines. Square footage runs from quite small to moderately large. Available as erected shell, rough finish house, or turnkey-ready. The company offers a "buyer's plan" granting a 2% discount for orders delivered at the manufacturer's convenience.

AMERICAN BARN (123 Elm Street, Deerfield, Massachusetts 01373). Simple buildings with barn-like exteriors "based on the original Old Deerfield, Mass., barn." Post and beam construction; rustic-looking interiors with heavy wooden beams. American Barn also offers a screened porch and a bedroom-garage wing. Sizes range from medium to moderately large; two-story barns and Cape Cods. Available as materials package, erected shell, rough finish, and turnkey-ready.

BOW HOUSE (Randall Road, Bolton, Massachusetts 01740). Bow House offers three Cape Cods, all beautifully detailed reproductions of a type of early New England home which had a bow roof—a curved roof offering more headroom than a Cape Cod and more subtlety than a gambrel roof. The homes include such authentic interior details as divided windows, plaster walls, brick floors, cedar clapboard siding, and a "good morning" staircase. Optional additions to the basic home are available. The homes are well thought out and carefully designed. If you want a colonial home that is worthy of the name, this is it. Fireplaces galore. Sizes range from medium to moderately large.

CONTINENTAL HOMES (Box 1800, Roanoke, Virginia 24008). Plants in Virginia and Missouri. Traditional designs with some "Southern" features in exteriors such as brick siding, porches, and full length windows. Standard plans with many variations. Many models with good-sized eat-in kitchens and formal dining rooms. The circulation patterns are well designed. Some of the larger models have two fireplaces. Sizes range from small to large.

CRAFTMARK HOMES (4595 Morgan Place, Liverpool, New York 13088). Marketed in New York, New Jersey, Pennsylvania, and Massachusetts. Traditional designs and standard floor plans. Some models have exteriors resembling New England farmhouses. Sizes range from small to medium.

DECK HOUSE (930 Main Street, Acton, Massachusetts 01720). A well-established company with a sales representative network offering homes sold mostly along the east coast, with some units going as far as California. Their homes are marked by an appealing simplicity and solid, sober contemporary design. Deck House products have a characteristic appearance because of the extensive use of natural woods, decks, large areas of glass, and a roof of cedar decking which creates a natural wood cathedral ceiling above the living room. Sizes range from medium to very large. Most plans are bi-levels with the upper floor living room opening onto a deck. The company considers plans presented in its literature as starting points from which company and buyer can proceed to a fully customized home. Materials are of very high quality.

(ACORN STRUCTURES, SAM ROBBINS)

(AMERICAN BARN)

(DECK HOUSE, FRED ROLA)

These homes are not inexpensive. Available as materials package, erected shell, or completed home. Post and beam construction.

FLEXI-PANEL (1000 Apache Boulevard, Tempe, Arizona 85281). This company markets its products nationwide and offers free delivery in Arizona. Theirs is an entire building system, with post and beam construction, "sandwich" wall panels, and self-contained plumbing panel wall for bathroom/kitchen. Flexi-Panel describes its homes as "low cost housing and summer homes," and they are available in kit form. However, the company suggests professional supervision if you plan to erect the shell yourself and further recommends that all electric, plumbing, and masonry work be done by skilled labor. Standard plans are for basic ranch houses in small to medium sizes which can be custom designed for your specific needs.

IVON R. FORD (McDonough, New York 13801). Marketed in New England and mid-Atlantic states by a dealer network. They offer traditional styles and a large variety of standard house plans, as well as vacation models. Ford homes are fully panelized and are described by the manufacturer as "up in a day." A crane is necessary on the site. Sizes range from small to medium.

GREAT NORTHERN HOMES (21 Worthen Road, Lexington, Massachusetts 02173). Vacation homes of contemporary design and "alpine" type (two-story houses with deep eaves overhang, "gingerbread," and such exterior trim as shutters and deck railings). Compact two-story plans in medium-size range.

HABITAT (123 Elm Street, Deerfield, Massachusetts 01373). Marketed in eastern United States. Vacation homes in a variety of styles such as A-frame, alpine, and prow (the front end walls meet at a point). Rustic interior details such as exposed beams and paneled walls with lots of glass, decks, and porches. These post and beam construction homes range in size from small to medium. The company is not to be confused with Moshe Safdie's Habitat design or apartment complex in Montreal.

HOMECRAFT (P. O. Box 35, South Hill, Virginia 23970). Sold in the seven-state area around Virginia by representatives and builder-dealers. Traditional styles and standard plans, with some "Southern" exterior details, such as columned porticos and full-length windows; some vacation models. Sizes range from small to large. Wall sections and roof trusses come preassembled.

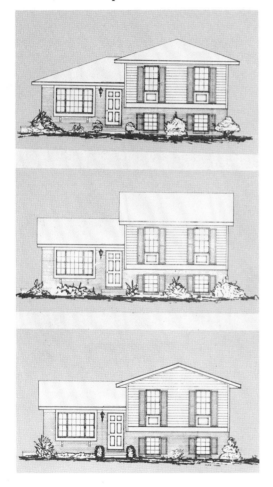

Variations on a split-level theme (HOME-CRAFT)

LEISURE HOMES (3609 Logangate Road, Youngstown, Ohio 44505). Typical vacation home styles—"chalet," cottage, and A-frame—with typical floor plans including sleeping lofts, decks, and porches. Two-story models with living room and kitchen on upper floors are also offered.

LINDAL CEDAR HOMES (Home Office: 10411 Empire Way South, Seattle, Washington 98178; plants in Washington, Canada, England, and Japan). Marketed throughout the United States (including Hawaii) and Canada by local distributors. Lindal produces a large variety of models using natural woods, especially cedar, for exteriors and interiors. Many year-round and vacation homes, including A-frames and alpines, are offered. Many have balconies and decks. Sizes range from very small to large. Post and beam construction. Lindal sells a materials package for the buyer to erect himself, using an erection manual and numbered parts. Some distributors may help you to find a professional builder. Packages are available in a selection of materials to meet your budget. Some of their homes are very striking indeed.

MILLER MANUFACTURING CO. (P. O. Box 1356, Richmond, Virginia 23211). Traditional style homes with such "Southern" details as columned porticos and an option for brick siding. Many models have front porches. Standard floor plans in sizes ranging from small to large. They sell a panelized package to a local contractor who erects the home on your site.

NATIONAL HOMES (P. O. Box 680, Lafayette, Indiana 47902). Marketed in 38 states east of the Rockies. A very large manufacturer of panelized homes. National offers homes that are primarily traditional in design with standard floor plans, but a large variety. Some models have options for exteriors that are more contemporary looking. Each of their many floor plans has two or more alternate exterior designs. Sizes range from small to large. National has commissioned several famous architects to design exteriors. They also offer a line of vacation homes.

NEW CENTURY HOMES (State Road 26 East, Lafayette, Indiana 47902). Sold within a 250-mile radius of Lafayette, Indiana, by a builder network. Traditional designs and standard floor plans; one vacation home model. Sizes range from small to large.

NEW ENGLAND HOMES (Freeman's Point, Portsmouth, New Hampshire 03801). Traditional styles with emphasis on New England variations such as saltboxes and gambrel roofs. Standard floor plans. Sizes range from small to medium. Some models have especially attractive and unusual details such as built-in bookshelves and a wood box near the fireplace. Their specifications list indicates good quality materials. The homes are panelized and require a crane for erection. The company sells the exterior shell package to a local builder rather than directly to the customer.

OMEGA STRUCTURES (134 Main Street, New Canaan, Connecticut 06840). These are simple, contemporary post and beam houses. Omega offers a complete component system with floor, wall, and roof panels; bath, kitchen, and closet units; "prefinished, pre-wired, and pre-plumbed." A crane is needed. Some standard plans are available, but the company will custom design for you using their system components. The construction system allows for great flexibility of size from small to very large. So flexible is the system that you can literally design your home yourself. The possibilities for exteriors are almost unlimited. We were especially impressed with the clean design of their homes. And their literature avoided the hard-sell jargon of some manufacturers, presenting their product calmly, completely, and understandably.

PAN ABODE (4350 Lake Washington Boulevard, North Renton, Washington 98055). Marketed throughout the United States, including Hawaii and Guam, by a dealer network, some of whom also act as contractors. The product is a log cabin built from a system of prenotched cedar logs which interlock at corners and are stacked to form the exterior walls. Because of the thickness of the logs, the exterior walls are self-insulating. The homes have a rustic look, both on the exterior and interior. Interior wall partitions are also of cedar logs, except the plumbing wall for the bathroom and kitchen. All models are single-story, the number of plans is limited, and the homes range in size from very small to medium. The company offers custom design services and encourages the buyer to build it himself. Pan Abode provides erection drawings.

RADEXHOMES (233 Sansome Street, San Francisco, California 94104). Marketed in the west through dealer representatives. The product is called the Hexaplex house, consisting of 12 triangular sections. The exterior walls and roof form a continuous structure, just as A-frames and geodesic domes are continuous. One basic style and size is offered but it can be expanded with projecting wings, a site-built understory (erecting the package on top of an above-ground block wall provides for a lower story), and an interior balcony. The interior has a strong sense of space and openness, and the basic model uses a great deal of glass. Radexhomes offers a materials kit, an erected shell, and a complete home package. A crane is required to erect the shell. The design is unique, attractive, practical, and for the more adventurous.

The Hexaplex home (RADEXHOMES)

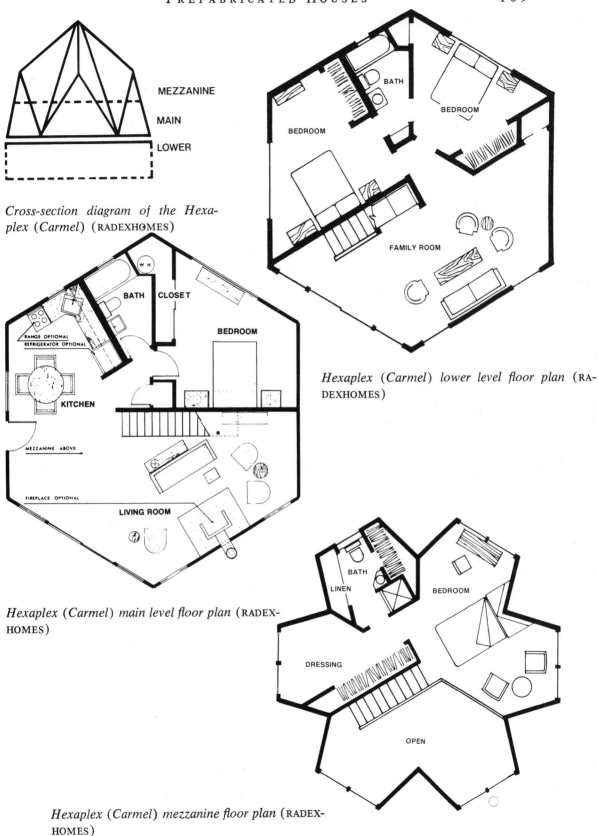

Cross-section diagram of the Hexaplex (Carmel) (RADEXHOMES)

MEZZANINE

MAIN

LOWER

BATH

BEDROOM

BEDROOM

FAMILY ROOM

Hexaplex (Carmel) lower level floor plan (RADEXHOMES)

W H

BATH   CLOSET

RANGE OPTIONAL
REFRIGERATOR OPTIONAL

BEDROOM

KITCHEN

MEZZANINE ABOVE

FIREPLACE OPTIONAL

LIVING ROOM

Hexaplex (Carmel) main level floor plan (RADEX-HOMES)

BATH

LINEN

BEDROOM

DRESSING

OPEN

Hexaplex (Carmel) mezzanine floor plan (RADEX-HOMES)

REASOR CORPORATION [*IBC Homes*] (500 West Lincoln, Charleston, Illinois 61920). Marketed within a 500-mile radius of its Mattoon, Illinois, plant. Standard floor plans with what the manufacturer calls traditional, colonial, conventional, modern, and provincial exteriors. Many of their homes have built-in garages. Sizes range from small to moderately large, and the manufacturer supplies an erected shell with studded partitions.

RIDGE HOMES (1100 Ridge Pike, Conshohocken, Pennsylvania 19428). Marketed in mid-Atlantic states, New England, and midwest by dealers in 14 states. Traditional designs with interchangeable exterior treatment options: roof types, windows, doors, siding materials. Four vacation models are available. Standard floor plans are offered, and the company encourages modifications for custom design. Sizes range from small to large. Especially attractive for the buyer seeking to do much of the work himself or to act as his own contractor. No unique design here. Ridge offers a semiconstructed home, that is, a weathertight shell on a basement with studded interior partition walls. They supply illustrated materials on how to install wiring, sheetrock and do other work yourself. Ridge offers its own financing, a single-purpose loan which covers construction, and a multi-purpose loan which covers the construction and can be extended to a 16-year mortgage.

"The Seville" by Scholz Homes, exterior view (SCHOLZ HOMES, DIVISION OF INLAND STEEL URBAN DEVELOPMENT CORP.)

"The Seville," interior view (SCHOLZ HOMES DIVISION OF INLAND STEEL URBAN DEVELOPMENT CORP.)

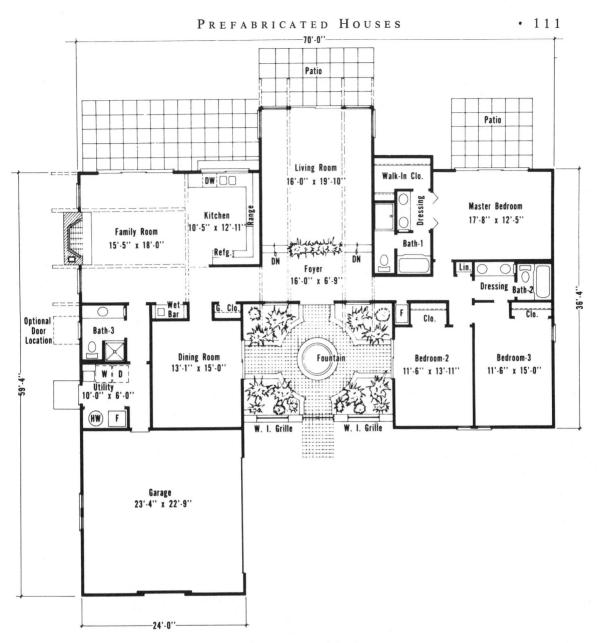

"The Seville," floor plan for one of several models (SCHOLZ HOMES DIVISION OF INLAND STEEL URBAN DEVELOPMENT CORP.)

SCHOLZ HOMES (2001 North Westwood, Toledo, Ohio 43607). Marketed in eastern United States by a network of sales representatives and builders. These homes can be quite expensive and are among the most sumptuous products of the prefabricated home industry. Scholz offers a variety of exterior design styles—traditional, contemporary, and several designs rare in prefabricated housing, such as their French chateau and Spanish colonial style. An especially large variety of floor plans with extensive customizing is available. Sizes range from small to very large and many of the homes have uncommon luxury details—spiral staircases, wet bar, sunken living room, bay windows, and many more options. They sell a package of rough and finish carpentry to the builder-dealer who erects the home for the customer. They are very well worth investigating if your budget is not tight and you have a taste for the truly elegant traditional home. Scholz homes are quite remarkable.

SPACEMAKERS (146 Will Drive, Canton, Massachusetts 02021). Marketed in the eastern United States, as far south as North Carolina and as far west as West Virginia by a network of salesmen and builder-dealers. They offer vacation homes in a variety of styles and floor plans, with typical vacation home features such as lofts, two-story cathedral ceilings, decks, balconies, glass walls, courtyard, etc. Sizes range from small to moderately large. Spacemakers' products are post and beam construction homes which emphasize natural wood finishes.

STANMAR (Boston Post Road, Sudbury, Massachusetts 01776). Primarily manufacturers of vacation homes, Stanmar's products are marketed throughout the United States, including the Virgin Islands and Puerto Rico, with the heaviest concentration in the northeast. We've seen a number of their homes in "leisure" communities in the Poconos of Pennsylvania. Stanmar sells its units through authorized dealers and approved builders. Post and beam construction; a variety of styles and floor plans. They offer a "lifetime home registration" plan; that is, they keep your plans and specifications on permanent file (which means for as long as the house stands or the manufacturer is in business, whichever is shorter).

TECHBUILT (323 North Main Street, Spring Valley, New York 10977). Marketed primarily in the east but Techbuilt homes have been built as far west as Denver, in Europe, and the Caribbean. This is one of the oldest names in prefabricated housing. The trio of Techbuilt and its two competitors, Acorn Structures and Deck Houses, are the principal proponents of the clean, simple, modern look in prefabricated year-round homes, stressing natural woods, glass, and well thought out floor plans. Techbuilt has won awards for architectural design. They

(SPACEMAKERS)

offer year-round and vacation homes, all with a distinctive look resulting from the use of brick, wood, beamed ceilings, etc. Many standard as well as some unusual floor plans. Custom designs built for others, some of which are shown in Techbuilt's literature, are also available. Post and beam construction; sizes range from small to very large; high quality materials; not for people on tight budgets.

UNIVERSAL MANUFACTURING [*Don Huber Homes*] (Camden, Ohio 45311). Marketed in Ohio and Indiana through franchised dealers. Traditional design with some vacation homes. Sizes range from small to moderately large. Standard floor plans for the smaller homes, but larger units have special features such as a library, two-room master bedroom "suite," dressing rooms, built-in bookcases. They supply a rough finish and interior trim package which they or a dealer can build.

VERMONT LOG BUILDINGS (Hartland, Vermont 05048; other plants in Mon-

tana and North Carolina). Marketed in the northeast, southeast, south central states, and Montana. The buyer can deal directly with the company or through a franchised dealer. The product is a log cabin system with notched logs for exterior walls. Vermont Log Buildings sells only exterior walls and the roof framing system, clearly aiming at the build-it-yourself market. They supply working blueprints, a construction manual, numbered pieces, and some field supervision. The company offers many options for varying floor plans—extensions, porches, dormers—and details that add to the "real" log cabin look, such as a "woodshed" projection that can be used as a bunk room, bathroom, or for storage. To have other structures on your property in keeping with a log cabin main house, the company also offers freestanding log cabin garages, barns, and sheds. A variety of plans are offered, but most are Cape Cods or gambrel roofs in sizes ranging from small to moderately large. A new product, Cluster Sheds, is

A log cabin home (VERMONT LOG BUILDINGS)

offered, that is 12′ × 16′ post and beam structures designed to be built by the buyer and arranged, singly or in multiples, as one attached structure. They can be built one at a time or all at once. These cluster sheds are the purest form of a prefabricated modular home system.

Cost Checklist

The list which follows is designed to help you calculate just what your costs will be and to help you to make valid comparisons between different manufacturers and models. We recommend that you make a copy of these pages and answer all questions for each and every model you are considering. Comparing all of the completed checklists should indicate, roughly, which manufac-

turer is offering the best price. The cost checklist should be used in conjunction with the materials checklist at the end of the specifications chapter.

1. The Building Lot

Land	$_____
Lawyer (including all contracts for land and home, searches, closing, and anticipated appearances before local boards)	$_____
Land survey (if recent survey is unavailable from seller)	$_____
Title insurance (one-time expense)	$_____
Land transfer taxes, if any	$_____
Building permit application fee	$_____
Building permit	$_____

Soil percolation test (if you are
   installing a septic system) $_____
Soil log (for septic system) $_____
Engineered septic design $_____
Septic system permit $_____
Well permit (if you have to dig
   your own well) $_____

2. The Prefabricated Home

Alternative #1
House materials package (in-
   cluding all options) $_____
All other materials not in-
   cluded in the package $_____
Labor costs for all work not
   done by buyer $_____
Transportation of package $_____

Alternative #2
Full materials package (in-
   cluding all options) $_____
Labor costs for all work not
   done by buyer $_____
Transportation of package $_____

Alternative #3
Cost of erected shell $_____
All other materials not included
   in package $_____
Labor costs for all additional
   work $_____
Transportation of package $_____

Alternative #4
Cost of rough finish house $_____
All other materials not included
   in package $_____
Labor costs for all additional
   work $_____
Transportation of package $_____

Alternative #5
Full cost of completed (turnkey-ready) home $_____

Taxes, if any, on purchase
   price $_____
Other necessary buildings (garage, carport, storage shed,
   etc.) $_____
Other exterior construction
   (stairs, patio, deck, etc.) $_____

3. Site Work

Land clearing, if necessary, to
   receive prefabricated home $_____
Preliminary grading $_____
Foundation (excavation and
   construction) $_____
Road or driveway construction
   (culverts, etc.) $_____
Road or driveway surface
   (stone, macadam) $_____
Installation of above-ground
   electrical service $_____
   or
Installation of underground
   electric service $_____
If underground and you pay
   for the trench, how much? $_____
If a transformer is required
   and you pay for it, how much? $_____
If the transformer requires a
   pad and you pay for it, how
   much? $_____
Electrical hookup from service
   line to home $_____
Installation of above-ground
   telephone service $_____
   Will the telephone company
   allow you to install underground service in the same
   trench with underground
   electrical service?
Telephone installation (equipment, receivers, service
   charge) $_____
Septic system built to prevailing
   specifications or better $_____
Plumbing and hook-up from
   septic system to home $_____
   or
Plumbing and hookup from
   home to existing public
   sewerage lines $_____
Cased-in well dug to prevailing
   specifications or better and
   desired water pressure $_____
Plumbing and hookup from
   well to home $_____
   or
Plumbing and hookup from
   public water supply to home $_____

Final grading $_____
Inspections $_____
Occupancy permit $_____

4. Other Expenses

Homeowner's insurance policy
on the home per year (usually
required by the lending institution) $_____
Budget for landscaping per year
(lawn, trees, shrubs, etc.) $_____
Estimated annual property taxes $_____
Other annual municipal taxes $_____
Estimate your annual maintenance costs (painting, cleaning, general repairs) $_____

5. Utilities

Estimate your monthly electric
bill $_____
Estimate your monthly gas bill $_____
Estimate your monthly fuel (for
heating) bill $_____
Estimate your monthly telephone bill $_____
Estimate your monthly garbage
collection bill if not provided
by the municipality $_____
Estimate your annual bill for
use of public sewerage lines $_____
Estimate your annual bill for use
of public water supply $_____

6. Money

How much money will you
need? $_____
How much money do you have? $_____
How much of the cash you have
in hand will you be supplying
as a down payment on the
prefabricated home? $_____

How large a mortgage will you
need? $_____
For how many years (when they
tell you the monthly payment,
you'll know how long a
period you'll need)?
For lending institutions (commercial banks, savings banks,
and savings and loan as-
sociations):
Will you need a conventional
mortgage or a construction
mortgage? At what interest
rate? (% per year) _____%
Is the interest rate "simple
interest" or "add-on" interest?
If "add-on" interest, what is
the "true interest" rate? % _____%
If the lending institution
charges a fee for processing
your application, how much? $_____
If the lending institution
charges "points," how much
will this cost? $_____
Are there any other one-time
fees or charges levied by the
institution and how much will
they cost? $_____
Does the lending institution
penalize you for the early repayment of the loan? If so,
what is the penalty? $_____
Does the monthly payment to
the lending institution include
all municipal taxes?
What is the total amount of
money you will pay for your
loan (the number of installments multiplied by the
monthly payment)? $_____
Of this amount, how much is
interest and fees (deduct the
principal borrowed from the
total amount of money you
pay the lending institution)? $_____

DOMES

(JOHN SOTO, *The New York Times*)

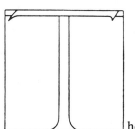he dome, an unusual prefabricated home, is at the same time one of the newest and one of the oldest forms of housing. The nomadic Mongolians built dome-like mobile homes of matted felt and skins called yurts*, and everyone knows what an Eskimo igloo looks like. The Bakinga Pygmies covered their domes with leaves, the people of Kenya used thatch. In South Africa, Guyana, the Cameroons, and the Arab world domes took other forms.

In the Western world, architects in Europe and Asia Minor associated the dome with heaven, and used it on many religious buildings, especially in the Mediterranean region. Among the classic domes are those on Hagia Sophia in Istanbul (completed in 63 A.D.), the Church of Saint George in Salonica (c. 310 A.D.), the Church of the Holy Sepulchre in Jerusalem (c. 348 A.D.), the Temple of Minerva in Rome (c. 350 A.D.), San Marco in Venice (c. 1094 A.D.), and the Orthodox Baptistry in Ravenna (5th century A.D.), as well as the Capitol in Washington, D.C., and other temples of government, the modern religion.

* Yurts are catching on as a form of housing. Several groups are providing a variety of services for those interested in building a yurt. One such group is the Yurt Foundation in Bucks Harbor, Maine, which offers two sets of plans for a nominal fee. Yurts are meant to be collapsed and moved.

A sixteenth-century print of an Indian village on the East Coast of Florida indicates that the Seminoles erected dome-like structures for homes. Longwood, the palatial residence near Natchez, Mississippi, begun in 1860, is capped with a dome. R. Buckminster Fuller's 1927 Dymaxion House, which was round and came to a point, evolved into his second Dymaxion House of 1947 and eventually led to the geodesic dome of today.

Fuller's enormous contribution to dome architecture, which enabled the form to be made practical for widespread use in a technological society, was the conception of the geodesic dome—material joined geometrically so that a maximum area is covered with a minimum of materials, creating in the process a structure that perhaps has the highest strength rating per weight of any structure heretofore conceived. Because the geodesic dome consists of individual parts—flat plane triangles which when attached form a series of curved pentagons; when these are bolted together they form a dome—these parts can be mass produced and assembled on a site in little time. This ease of construction is translated into substantial savings to the consumer. Because the dome can be erected with unskilled labor, a still greater saving can be achieved.

A membrane-covered dome showing the geodesic structure (DOME EAST)

Fuller domes have been built by native workers in the hills of Afghanistan and skilled labor in the suburbs here at home. In his book *Ideas and Integrities** he relates how a native work force in Kabul took 48 hours to erect a 10,000-square-foot dome with aluminum tubes, hubs, and a skin of stretched vinyl while their more "skilled" union counterparts in St. Louis took a month and a half at $5.50 an hour to erect the identical structure. In the United States, Fuller concluded, we incorrectly assume that anyone building a home must be a skilled craftsman.

What we assume Fuller means to tell us with this story is that the dome builder, working with friends, can erect the structure at a much cheaper cost and with the same degree of expertise than would be the case with a hired professional crew paid at union scale.

For the erection of the twin 39′ domes

* New York: Collier Books, 1969, p. 281.

in which we have lived for more than four years, we held an old-fashioned house raising. We invited a group of friends, and among us we erected the exterior of both domes, which enclose 2200 square feet of area, in a little more than 10 hours. Our cost for labor amounted to two cases of beer and about 30 pounds of hamburger and frankfurters. Add to this the fun and great joy of building one's home with one's friends.

Domes have a number of advantages:

1. *Cost.* Domes, on the whole, cost less per square foot than conventional and many prefabricated homes: the shell is easy to erect; the structure is self-supporting (no expensive posts and beams or weight-bearing walls); and the structure's walls are their own roofs (no expensive roof construction or roofing). Our turnkey-ready dome in rural New Jersey cost a little more than half

the cost of a conventional, stick-built home with the same area.

2. *Ease of construction.* Kits are easy to construct yourself, but unless you have proven building skills, the foundation, plumbing, heating, wiring, and interior carpentry require skilled labor. Building a dome from scratch—calculating the geometry, cutting, and assembling each of the triangles—is very difficult.

3. *Interior design flexibility.* As domes are self-supporting, you can plan whatever floor space you wish. The dome can be left entirely open, or rooms in any configuration can be built. The entirely open structure will be just as strong as one with interior walls.

4. *Spaciousness.* Domes can be as spacious or as enclosed as desired. The most commonly used residential dome is 39′ in diameter at its widest point at ground level and about 16′ high at its center, providing 1100 square feet of space with a volume of 12,000 cubic feet.

5. *One or two stories.* The 39′ dome and domes of other sizes are high enough to have a second story. A full second story will not allow for the feeling of dome living at ground level, for the ceiling would be about 8′ high and cut off the view to the top of the dome. To compensate for this, some dome owners have built a partial second story, so that a portion of the dome is entirely open and the balance is enclosed. A second story increases the economy of the structure. Weight-bearing walls will have to be constructed to support the second story, however.

6. *Tremendous strength.* The weight load for the dome's surface is very high, making domes attractive forms of housing in those parts of the country receiving heavy snow.

7. *Wind resistance.* Because of their roundness, domes have a greater ability to withstand high wind velocity than vertical structures, which makes them attractive in hurricane and tornado zones.

8. *Acoustics.* Music sounds spectacular in an open dome. You get the feeling of being within the group of performers, wherever you might be in the dome. However, there are some sounds that you might not like to have amplified.

9. *Natural light.* The 39′ dome—which is not round, but a decagon at the base with five 8′ sides alternating with five 16′ sides—has five trapezoidal openings around the base on the 16′ sides where windows or glass doors can be placed. Therefore, five different exposures are available to capture a great deal of natural light and natural heat throughout the year. Further, each of these trapezoidal openings can have glass doors (or any other kind of door) to provide entry in any or all of five locations. Most of the 39′ domes now being constructed also contain ten skylights that allow sunlight and solar heat to enter from above.

10. *The Elements.* Given some wind, snow will slide off the surface of the dome. Rain, too, will not accumulate on a dome as it might on a flat roof.

11. *Unique design.* To some, this is an important advantage. A dome is unique, it is ingenious, it is comfortable, and it is far from boring. The angles and interior configurations always offer visual fascination, and the exterior seems to blend with the

Workers and watchers at the authors' dome-raising

land upon which it sits, more than a traditional home that suddenly rises at a right angle from the land.

Here are some of the disadvantages.

1. *Code conformity.* Because the dome is unusual, you may have trouble getting the approval of the municipality and building inspector. Chances are good that your local building code does not specify standards of dome construction. Most dome manufacturers supply engineering drawings and other information needed to help demonstrate the building's structural soundness to the local authorities. In our case, the local building code specified only standard frame construction homes, but it allowed the building inspector to approve forms of housing not specifically mentioned at his discretion.

2. *Weatherproofing.* Many domes leak. Worse than aggravation and embarrassment is the damage unwanted water can cause to sheetrock walls, flooring, and the structure itself. Each manufacturer claims to have solved the problem—and the one you deal with may have—but the fact is that many domes leak. In our case, the domes were sealed by the general contractor, Geodesic Industries (also known at one time as Geodesic Structures) who are located in New Jersey. However, they failed to seal the domes properly. Water has caused damage of close to $6,000. Dome owners have used chemical coatings and shingles to prevent leaks. We used that oldest of methods—tar and webbing (one coat of tar, webbing placed above it, and a second coat of tar)—which has been completely successful. The tar webbing was placed over all seams, the blackness of the tar accentuating the geometry of the dome.

3. *Labor.* Though total costs will probably be less for a dome than for other forms of housing, several items will be more expensive, and work on the interior is one of them. The exterior frame of virtually all houses consists of four right angles; dome exteriors have no right angles. All materials for home construction are geared for right-angle structures, which means that you will have much more cutting and waste as you work with the complicated angles of the dome. The foundation, interior walls where they join the dome, and floors are the areas where labor will be most expensive.

4. *Acoustics.* As we indicated among the advantages, the acoustical properties can also be a disadvantage.

5. *Wall space.* Every home has two kinds of walls—exterior walls (one side of which is exposed to the elements, and the other side is inside the home) and interior walls (both sides are within the home). In a conventional home including all forms of manufactured housing with the exceptions of A-frames, the second floors of Cape Cods, gambrels, saltboxes, and the Hexaplex home, the exterior walls rise at a 90-degree angle from the ground. Furniture, almost all of which is square, can be placed against these walls with no loss of space, and art can be hung from them. In a dome, where the exterior walls curve inward, placement of square furniture against these walls creates some useless space between the base of the object and the wall. If your dome is large enough, you might find that you have adequate interior wall space and do not have to place anything against the curving exterior walls.

Building the Dome

The primary differences among manufacturers are in the quality of materials used, the sealing system for weatherproofing, the type of insulation, the design of the "hub" (the piece that creates the joint where the frame members come together), the braces of the triangles, the geometry itself, and, to some extent, the cost. An important factor is the location of the manufacturer's plant in relation to your building site, espe-

The spaciousness of the dome is evident as is the amount of natural light provided by the skylights (JOHN SOTO, *The New York Times*)

cially if you ask the manufacturer to do a portion of the construction. Not long ago manufacturers were asking $1 per mile per load (no one indicated what a "load" is or how many "loads" constituted one dome) to transport a kit.

A geodesic dome is constructed of wooden or metal framing pieces joined together at various angles to form a dome shape, with a skin of canvas, plastic, wood, or a combination of these materials placed over the frame.

The most logical way to buy a kit is in the form of pre-assembled panels (consisting of two right-angle triangles bolted together at the factory) with the skin attached and perhaps with a poured insulation in place. You can also use standard fiberglass batts for insulation between the framing members, but its square shape will force some waste because of the dome's unusual angles.

One company, Dome East, offers an unusual exterior-interior wall system, which they call a "sandwich." Unlike standard dome panels—which have the exterior skin in place but which require the installation of the interior finish wall and which also may require the installation of insulation— the Dome East "sandwich" consists of a prepainted piece of laminated aluminum ($\frac{1}{32}''$) attached to a sheet of plywood ($\frac{3}{16}''$) to which is attached $1\frac{7}{16}''$ rigid insulation and another sheet of plywood ($\frac{5}{32}''$) with wood paneling. No exterior painting, no insulation installation, no interior paneling or painting is needed. It sounds attractive.

The same company will also sell a set of hubs and working drawings from which to cut your own framing members and skin panels if you do not wish to buy a kit of pre-assembled panels. However, this cutting is very exact and we do not advise it if you do not have the necessary skills and tools.

If you purchase a kit and the manufacturer is not the general contractor, you will have much to do. You will be responsible for land, utilities, and services as well as foundation, interior carpentry, flooring, wiring, plumbing, heating, appliances, fixtures, and interior and exterior painting. Make sure you know exactly what is provided by the manufacturer when he quotes a kit price.

Being able to do a large part of the work is an advantage to some, for costs are lower and a heated, enclosed shelter can be built inexpensively, with the finishing touches being added later. Bearing in mind that some municipalities may not allow you to do some of the work, we advise that you check local building codes to make sure that what you want to do yourself is permitted.

Close-up of one manufacturer's hub and a hub with connecting struts is assembled into dome framework (DOME EAST)

Skilled labor may be provided by the manufacturer. If not, the manufacturer will provide the necessary architectural drawings for you or your contractor to follow. Dome East offers four levels of involvement: (1) they will sell the hubs and working drawings for you to do all the cutting and all subsequent work; (2) they will sell a kit for the shell, with all parts precut and instructions for assembly; (3) they will erect the kit you buy with their own crew or will send a supervisor to oversee construction if you do it yourself; (4) they will do the entire job, acting as general contractor and producing a turnkey-ready dome.

If we could erect the shell with friends so can you, for none of us had any building skills. One company estimates 100 man-hours to erect a 39' ⅜ dome and 60 man-hours for a 26' dome. This presupposes that each panel is fully assembled—frames, braces, and skin in one unit with pre-drilled holes for the bolts (to attach the triangles together), and proper location of anchor bolts marked. Anchor bolts attach to the foundation and hold the structure down; they are installed when the foundation is prepared. You need but three items: (1) manpower (yourself and at least three friends); (2) socket wrenches; (3) scaffolding that can be moved (for the high parts of the structure). No carpentry is needed to erect the shell, unless the panels have been improperly made. However, carpentry skills or a carpenter will be necessary for construction of the interior framing for walls, partitions, closets, and so forth.

You should have no difficulty acting as your own contractor. No special, unusual skills are needed to build a dome. The excavator and mason should have no problem with the foundation if they follow, exactly, the forms for the angles provided by the manufacturer, or if they make the forms themselves from the manufacturer's blueprint. The same is true for the electrician and plumber. Electrical wiring will pass through the triangles' studding just as it would through traditional wall studs. Plumbing lines will be installed in the traditional way if the domes are set above a crawl space or basement, or will be placed beneath the slab. The flooring people—whether they are installing wood floors, linoleum, tiles, or carpeting—will complain some about the angles, and the people doing the sheetrock will complain, too, but these are minor matters.

Domes sold commercially for residences are ⅜, ½, ⅝, or ¾ of a sphere. A full geodesic dome, like Fuller's United States Pavilion at Expo '67 in Montreal, would be a complete sphere. The greater the fraction of the sphere, given the same diameter, the higher the dome will be. Height is important if you are planning a second or even third story.

Domes have the flexibility of prefabricated homes in that they can be placed over a basement, be raised somewhat off the ground, or go atop a slab or crawl space. Use of a basement will double the amount of area. Use of a wall—the wall is built on the foundation and the dome is erected on top of the wall—will raise the height of the dome, perhaps giving more room for additional interior stories. These walls—called "risers"—would, for example, give more room for a second story in a 39' ⅜ dome.

Manufacturers offer a variety of openings which can be placed within the trapezoids created by the geometry of the dome. These include standard hinged doors, standard double-hung windows, sliding glass doors, or solid wood if you need the opening for wall space. Windows and doors offered are all standard items and are rectangular in shape. The openings are 8' high with 16' at the base and 8' at the top; the trapezoid thus formed creates an 8' x 8' square flanked on both sides by right angle triangles (generally called "wings") with 4'-bases. In our home we installed 8' x 8' sliding insulated glass doors in each opening; the wing panels are all of wood except for the entrance, where we used insulated glass which had to be specially made.

Glass or plastic can be installed elsewhere on the dome, provided you do not cut through any of the framing members, for doing so would affect the structural integrity of the dome.

1. Dome panels awaiting erection   2. Two men lift the first panel   3. The first panel is anchored to the foundation   4. Bolting panels together with a socket wrench   5. Attaching panels on upper part of dome from a scaffold

A canopy extending from the top and sides of the trapezoidal openings adds visual interest and some weather protection for the glass. However, unless the canopy is properly constructed it can create annoying drips during rains. Our canopies drip badly. It is like walking through a sheet of water to get inside or outside.

A word about skylights. Clear plastic or glass will provide maximum sunlight and solar heat. In warm climates, or in those parts of the country where the heat during some times of the year is especially high, clear skylights may not be desirable. We were concerned that too much heat would enter through the skylights during the hot summer months, so we installed opaque plastic skylights. The skylights generally used by dome manufacturers generally consist of two panels per skylight, one on the exterior of the shell and one seen from inside the structure. By using opaque skylights for each sheet, we cut the heat and light substantially. The exterior opaque panel reduces light and heat by 25% and the interior opaque panel takes 25% out of that, so we get 56% of the sunlight and heat.

If you are planning areas with large amounts of glass, we again recommend using insulated glass, for it will keep the dome warmer in winter (and reduce your heating bills) and cooler in summer (and reduce your air conditioning bills, if you have them) and will not sweat as single-pane glass will in winter.

We found that we do not need air conditioning, because the glass doors in each of the trapezoidal openings, when open, capture breezes and offer superb cross ventilation. Don't forget to order screens.

The Kit

Your kit will probably have the following items: basic shell (framing and skin panels), insulation, doors, windows, and the triangular wing panels for the openings, canopies and other light openings such as skylights and transoms, possibly paneling for the interior walls, and last but not least, a sealing system for weatherproofing.

The sealing system is critical. In our case, the people at Geodesic Industries caulked all seams between the triangles and then

A dome on a riser wall (DOME EAST)

placed a Celastic tape soaked with acetone over the seams. This system was to have formed an impenetrable bond. It was a glorious failure. The tape curled, the acetone did not properly bond. Whatever tiny holes might exist, we were told, would be filled once the coat of primer paint and the two coats of exterior-grade house paint were applied. This was not to be.

The house leaked like a sieve at the first rain, bringing all of our pots and pans into service. The contractors came to do spot patching with Celastic tape and acetone, to no avail. After a year of living in a leaking dome, we filed suit against the builder, went through arbitration from which we received a substantial award, and have been waiting for close to four years for a resolution of the suit.

We were in a poor position vis-à-vis the use of a chemical sealant. Manufacturers of these sealants were very reluctant to sell us their products because they were concerned that their sealants would not bond properly over seams already covered with Celastic tape, hardened acetone, one coat of primer, and two coats of house paint. Were it not for a local builder who suggested and applied tar with webbing, our domes would still leak.

Tar on seams provides weatherproofing and accentuates the structural geometry

Because of the consequences to the interior from unwanted water, improper sealing can be a dome's downfall. One company, in its brochure, did not even mention sealants. Another specified "Miracle Adhesive Tape, Imron caulking, and a prime coat of paint"—which sounds like trouble. A third specified Neoprene and Hypalon, synthetic coatings of rubber, about which we have heard good things.

Whichever sealant you use, remember that it must be sufficiently flexible to expand and contract with changing weather conditions, as the wood used in the shell expands and contracts.

One absolutely reliable sealing method is still the old, tried and true layers of shingles or shakes on felt, attached by nails to the surface of the dome. It is an expensive solution: the materials are expensive to begin with, and the surface to be covered is much larger than that of a conventional roof.

Another precaution to take is to use a high-grade caulk between each of the triangles. Our contractor bought the cheapest caulk he could find, we later discovered.

Special precautions should be taken with skylights, transoms, or wherever you substitute a glass or plastic panel for the wood skin. Seal these areas carefully and heavily, for these joints are the most likely to leak, especially if a portion of these windows/skylights is higher or lower than the surface of the skin, creating crevices where water might collect if it does not run off properly.

Planning the Interior

The two most common sizes for residential domes are 39' and 26' in diameter. One can build one 39' dome or several, or even one 39' dome with several 26' domes attached, on slabs or crawl space or riser walls or basements. As a point of economy, it is less expensive to build one large dome than several smaller-sized ones.

The 39' ⅜ dome has 1,100 square feet and a height of slightly more than 16'; a 39' ⅝ dome will have the same area but a

A cedar shingled dome with triangular windows (DOME EAST)

height of 23'. The 26' dome comes in ½ and ¾ spheres; the ½ sphere is 13' high, the ¾ 18½'; both have 530 square feet of area at ground level.

The greater the height of the structure, the more headroom for a second story or loft. The 26' ¾ dome would provide about 300 square feet upstairs, the 39' ⅝ about 600 square feet. These figures apply to full second stories; partial lofts would have less area.

A two-dome house requires two foundations and two kits, etc., but only one mechanical system, and you receive the benefit of twice the floor space at ground level. An entirely open dome requires you to heat the full cubic volumes (12,000 cubic feet for the ⅜ 39' dome), and as heated air rises it may be expensive to maintain a warm area at ground level. A second story and rooms with walls and ceilings will keep heat in, and if you use electric heat, you place individual thermostats in each area to further control and conserve heat.

You might be interested in cubic footages. A 26' ½ sphere has 4,600 cubic feet; a 26' ¾ sphere has 7,300 cubic feet; a 39' ⅜ sphere has 12,000 cubic feet; a 39' ⅝ sphere has 19,600 cubic feet; a 49' ⅜ sphere has 20,600 cubic feet. There is a 60' dome that is more than 29' high, but it does not strike

us as reasonable for housing purposes. It has 2,800 square feet at ground level and, depending on the number of floors, a potential of 7,000 to 9,000 square feet.

The ground floor plan of any dome offers unlimited variations. Your walls can be free-standing or attached to the shell, and they can be placed wherever you want them. However, a second story or loft will rest upon the framing below it, and the wall will have to be built as a weight-bearing wall.

Geodesic domes also lend themselves to future expansion, for additional domes can readily be added and connected at the existing trapezoidal openings, without having to cut into the shell itself.

The manufacturer will probably offer some assistance with floor planning if you so request, and we will not delve into this aspect in great detail. A few points should be kept in mind.

Except at the openings, all exterior walls slope inwards and cannot be used in the traditional manner for hanging pictures; square furniture placed against these walls will create some useless space between the base of the furniture and the wall. Large pieces of furniture, bookcases, and art should be planned, if possible, for the interior walls, which are vertical. Passageways and halls should not be arranged at the

Two 39' domes joined (GEORGE R. SMITH, COURIER-NEWS)

perimeter of the domes unless you can afford to make them wider than usual to allow for sufficient headroom.

You also will find that the long, low construction of baseboard heat units will fit very conveniently where the floor meets the exterior walls, especially as it is not advisable to put anything against these walls anyway. And keeping the exterior walls free and clear allows one to better enjoy the geometry of the dome.

To keep noise transmission down in a structure which amplifies sound, you might have fiberglass insulation installed in interior partition walls or you can use acoustic tiles for the walls and ceilings.

As for fenestration (the design and location of windows), restrict yourself to the 16' trapezoidal openings, which is by no means a hindrance as these openings occupy ⅔ of the ⅜ dome's perimeter at the base.

Interior walls can be covered by any materials you wish—plywood paneling (we used ¼″ plywood for the interior of the shell), sheetrock (we used sheetrock for all interior partition walls), sprayed foam (some foams are highly flammable; most sprayed foam can be painted), etc. Plywood and sheetrock must be cut to fit the unusual

shapes of the dome. Plywood, because of its grain and because two pieces of plywood together do not make an invisible seam, tends to accentuate the interior geometry. Sheetrock, which when spackled and taped does make invisible seams, softens the geometry. The most continuous surface would be sprayed foam.

Lay your flooring before the interior partition walls are finished with sheetrock or plywood so that the flooring people can leave ragged edges which will be covered over by the finish wall and trim. The smaller the unit of flooring (tile, wood panel, etc.) the less wastage you will have.

Fireplaces, especially freestanding units, work well in domes. If you place the fireplace on the perimeter of the dome, the exterior flue will rise from the base of the dome to above the highest point of the dome. You might not find this to your taste. Furthermore, you will have to brace the flue to make sure that it will withstand high winds. If you locate the fireplace close to the center of the dome, the principal length of flue will be inside and only a short exterior length will be needed to bring the chimney above the peak of the dome. Metal freestanding fireplaces are excellent units, for they are not

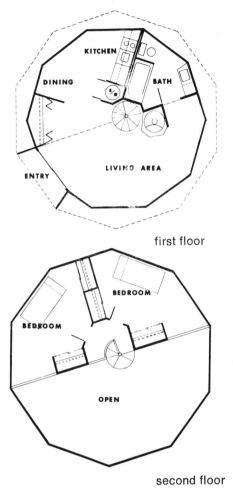

first floor

second floor

Possible plan for a ground floor and balcony of a single 26' dome (DOME EAST)

only attractive, but also throw a great deal of heat. Make sure that the unit is not too close to walls, draperies, books, records, or tapes, for the heat may do some damage. Give the unit plenty of room.

Costs

Unlike some other forms of manufactured housing, where a total package is offered, there are too many options available to the dome owner to provide meaningful cost comparisons. The only true comparison you can make is of the total kit price for a similar dome made by various manufacturers, again evaluating the materials to understand any

differentials. Also, you generally buy only the shell from the dome manufacturer. If the manufacturer also offers a turnkey-ready home, then you can readily compare your total costs against those of other forms of housing within this book.

Here is a rule of thumb offered by Cathedralite: The cost of the dome package, unassembled, is 25% to 35% of your total building costs, exclusive of land, foundation, utilities, and services. Costs of dome kits

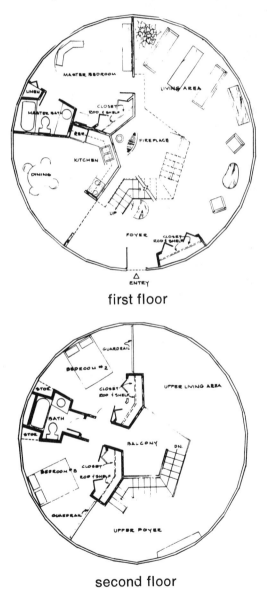

first floor

second floor

Possible plan for a ground floor and balcony of a single 39' dome (DOME EAST)

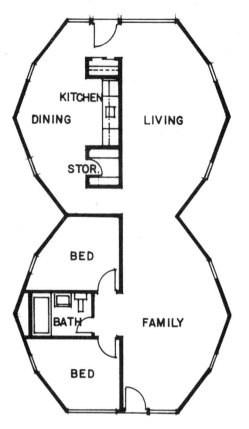

Possible plan for a two 26'-dome home (CATHEDRALITE)

have been rising along with other forms of housing. In 1972 a 39′ ⅜ sphere dome kit, without windows and doors, cost $3,500; two years later the same kit sold for about $9,000.

We have a strong suspicion that the economies which we were lucky enough to have four years ago may no longer apply. Domes now may be only competitive with others forms of prefabricated housing rather than considerably cheaper.

Financing

Banks have two principal concerns when you walk through the door with plans and estimates in hand: can you afford to meet the monthly payments, and if you default, will the bank be able to sell the home easily to get its money back?

Clearly, you will be able to show that you are getting a lot of house for the money. In our case, the bank, widely considered to be the most conservative lending institution in the county, gave us a preliminary approval within three days. Our plans were discussed at a board meeting and the loan was ap-

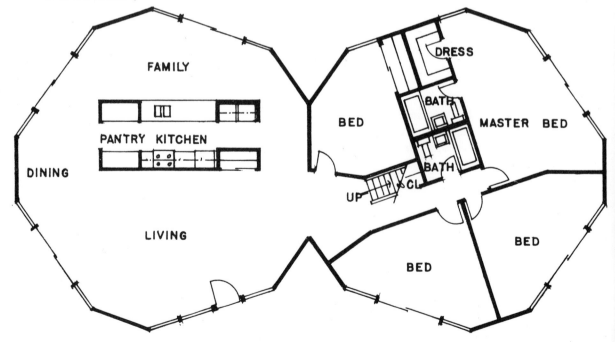

Possible plan for a two 39'-dome home (CATHEDRALITE)

proved immediately thereafter. Our banker was well aware of the size of the structure, the cost per square foot (no other building could approach this low figure), and the fact that our land equaled in value, or came close to, the amount of money we wanted to borrow.

Domes, like other permanent homes, appreciate with time. We consider them good investments that also provide comfort, shelter, and interesting surroundings.

Conclusion

Do we recommend domes? We sure do. But make sure that the manufacturer, be he the supplier of the kit or the general contractor, is reputable, that he stands by his product and workmanship, and that he makes necessary repairs within a reasonable period of time. Or to put it another way, we hope that the manufacturer and/or contractor you deal with will be the reverse of the people we dealt with.

Manufacturers

Dome manufacturers are, in general, much smaller operations than manufacturers of other forms of housing. Some of the printed materials they send in response to inquiries give minimal information, and it may take months to have questions answered, if they are answered at all. Several years ago there were mutterings about suits by one manufacturer against another for infringements of patents, and we don't know whether these issues are still up in the air (our letters weren't answered).

Here is a list of manufacturers that have, in some way, answered our inquiries. We have included the information we received. We do not recommend the people who were contractors on our domes, and they are not listed here.

CADCO OF NEW YORK STATE (Plattsburgh, New York 12901) manufactures 26′ and 39′ domes and also provides forms for pouring a slab and for the foundation. Their kit consists of panels which have been pre-assembled. They recommend 3″ of fiberglass insulation in colder climates.

CATHEDRALITE (P. O. Box B, Daly City, California 94017) manufactures 26′, 39′, and 60′ domes. The dome kit consists of pre-assembled triangles with a finished exterior, and they quote prices on insulation and a riser wall.

DOME EAST (325 Duffy Avenue, Hicksville, New York 11801) offers domes in four stages of completion: a connector (hubs) kit and you cut your own panels; a shell kit; an erected shell kit; a turnkey ready dome. They do not offer pre-assembled panels. They are also producing the "sandwich panel" system, described earlier. Their domes have membranes (i.e., vinyl or canvas) or solid panels (i.e., wood). Dome East offers a number of different structures and will custom design for residential, industrial, and commercial uses.

DYNA-DOME (22226 N. 23rd Avenue, Phoenix, Arizona 85027) offers 26′, 40′, 49′, 60′, and 70′ domes. A connector kit with plans for framing members and plywood skin or a shell kit can be purchased. They do not offer doors and windows. Dyna-Dome estimates transportation costs at between $4 and $10 per hundred pounds (depending on destination); a shell kit weighs about 4½ pounds per square foot of living area. These domes have a different geometry, with four openings per dome rather than the more common five openings.

GEODESIC DOMES (10290 Davison Road, Davison, Michigan 48423) referred us to their office in Plattsburgh, New York (see Cadco above). They seem to sell an A-frame unit which is meant to be attached to a dome opening. These units are available in sizes of 651, 976, and 1302 square feet.

ZOMEWORKS (P. O. Box 712, Albuquerque, New Mexico 87103) considers its marketing area to be New Mexico, Texas, and California. They do not list fixed prices; they design the structure with the customer and then manufacture the panels at an agreed upon price. They offer anything from "assembled skeleton panels with bolts, foundation plan and cardboard demonstration model" to a completed building. They also offer a solar heating system with insulated windows, a "skylid" ("Insulated louvers open when the sun shines and close during nighttime and periods of heavy overcast"; operated by freon cannisters), and solar heater. Zomes have vertical walls, making them structures with dome roofs rather than pure domes. Zomeworks has an aluminum panel similar to that described in the Dome East paragraph above. They also sell books and posters.

Cost Checklist

This checklist is designed to help you calculate just what your costs will be and to help you compare different manufacturers and products. We recommend that you make a copy of these pages and answer all questions for each dome you are considering. Comparing all of the completed checklists should indicate, roughly, which manufacturer is offering the best price. The cost checklist should be used in conjunction with the materials checklist at the end of the specifications chapter.

1. The Building Lot

Land $_____
Lawyer (including all contracts for land and home, searches, closing, and anticipated appearances before local boards) $_____
Land survey (if recent survey unavailable from seller) $_____
Title insurance (one-time expense) $_____
Land transfer taxes, if any $_____
Building permit application fee $_____
Building permit $_____
Soil percolation test (if you are installing a septic system) $_____
Soil log (for septic system) $_____
Engineered septic system $_____
Septic system permit $_____

Well permit (if you have to dig your own well) $_____

2. The Dome(s)

Dome(s) basic kit $_____
If the manufacturer is the general contractor, cost of the turnkey ready dome(s) $_____
If the manufacturer is not the general contractor, itemize the following costs:
Transportation of kit to site $_____
Cost of shell erection $_____
Wall framing (interior):
    Materials $_____
    Labor $_____
Finished walls (sheetrock, paneling, etc.):
    Materials $_____
    Labor $_____
Interior doors:
    Materials $_____
    Labor $_____
Closet doors:
    Materials $_____
    Labor $_____
Cabinetry and closets:
    Materials $_____
    Labor $_____
Insulation:
    Materials $_____
    Labor $_____
Windows and exterior doors:
    Materials $_____
    Labor $_____
Floor framing (not needed with slabs)
    Materials $_____
    Labor $_____
Flooring:
    Materials $_____
    Labor $_____
Electrical wiring:
    Materials $_____
    Labor $_____
Electrical fixtures:
    Materials $_____
    Labor $_____
Plumbing:

Materials (rough and finish plumbing) $_____

Labor (rough and finish) $_____

Plumbing fixtures:

Materials $_____

Labor $_____

Major appliances (refrigerator, stove-oven, dishwasher, clothes washer, clothes dryer) $_____

Heating system:

Materials (baseboard, furnace radiators) $_____

Labor $_____

Other requirements:

Materials $_____

Labor $_____

Total payment due dome manufacturer $_____

Taxes, if any, on purchase price $_____

Other necessary buildings (garage, carport, storage sheds, etc.) $_____

Other exterior construction (stairs, patio, deck, etc.) $_____

3. Site Work

Land clearing, if necessary, to receive the kit $_____

Preliminary grading $_____

Foundation (excavation and construction) $_____

Slab, if any $_____

Road or driveway construction (culverts, etc.) $_____

Road or driveway surface (stone, macadam) $_____

Installation of above-ground electric service $_____

or

Installation of underground electric service $_____

If underground and you pay for the trench, how much? $_____

If a transformer is required and you pay for it, how much? $_____

If the transformer requires a pad and you pay for it, how much? $_____

Electrical hookup from service line to home $_____

Installation of above-ground telephone service $_____

Will the telephone company allow you to install underground service in the same trench with underground electric service?

Telephone installation (equipment, receivers, service charge) $_____

Septic system to prevailing specifications or better $_____

Plumbing and hook-up from septic system to home $_____

or

Plumbing and hookup from public sewerage lines to home $_____

Cased-in well dug to prevailing specifications or better and desired water pressure $_____

Plumbing and hookup from well to home $_____

or

Plumbing and hookup from public water supply to home $_____

Final grading $_____

Inspections $_____

Occupancy permit $_____

4. Other Expenses

Homeowner's insurance policy on the dome per year (usually required by the lending institution) $_____

Budget for landscaping per year (lawn, trees, shrubs, etc.) $_____

Estimated annual property taxes $_____

Other annual municipal taxes $_____

Estimate your annual maintenance costs (painting, cleaning, general repairs) $_____

5. Utilities

Estimate your monthly electric bill $_____

Estimate your monthly gas bill $_____

Estimate your monthly fuel (for heating) bill $_____

Estimate your monthly telephone bill $_____

Estimate your monthly garbage collection bill if not provided by the municipality $_____

Estimate your annual bill for the use of public sewerage lines $_____

Estimate your annual bill for the use of public water supply $_____

6. Money

How much money will you need? $_____

How much money do you have? $_____

How much of the cash you have in hand will you be applying as a down payment on the dome? $_____

How large a mortgage will you need? $_____

For how many years (when they tell you the monthly payment you'll know how long a period you'll need)? $_____

For lending institutions (commercial banks, savings banks, and savings and loan associations):

Will you need a conventional mortgage or a construction mortgage? At what interest rate per year? $_____

Is the interest rate "simple interest" or "add-on" interest? If "simple interest," what is the rate? ____%

If "add-on" interest, what is the "true interest" rate (% per year)? ____%

If the lending institution charges a fee for processing your application, how much? $_____

If the lending institution charges "points", how much will this cost? $_____

Are there any other one-time fees or charges levied by the institution and how much will they cost? $_____

Does the lending institution penalize you for the early repayment of the loan? If so, what is the penalty? $_____

Does the monthly payment to the lending institution include all municipal taxes?

What is the total amount of money you will pay for your loan (the number of installments multiplied by the monthly payment)? $_____

Of this amount, how much is interest and fees (deduct the principal borrowed from the total amount of money you pay the lending institution)? $_____

SPECIFICATIONS

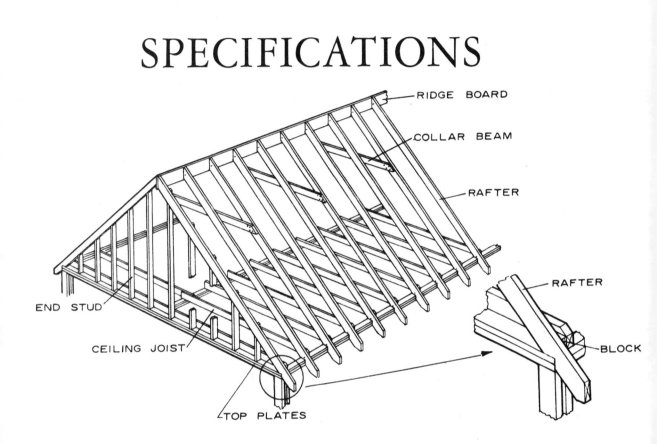

RIDGE BOARD

COLLAR BEAM

RAFTER

END STUD

CEILING JOIST

TOP PLATES

RAFTER

BLOCK

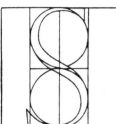pecifications are a critical part of your decision to buy a home. Each manufacturer offers a listing of the materials used in his homes. This list should be compared with the requirements of the local building code, and you should also compare specifications lists of different manufacturers to see which offers the best product at the best price.

Some manufacturers are explicit about materials, giving thicknesses of wood among other details. Other manufacturers use vague terms which are meaningless but which appear to be informative, such as "large closets" (how large is "large"?), or they may give the brand name of, say, a water heater but not indicate its capacity. You should question any specification that is insufficient. This chapter will describe the basic elements of construction as well as standards and types of materials and machinery.

Almost all manufacturers "reserve" the right to substitute materials or brand name items. It is imperative that you know exactly what *will* be used in your home, not what *may* be used. For example, there may not be much difference between two refrigerators of the same type with the same capacity, but there is enormous difference between structural grade Douglas fir and utility grade hemlock.

Among the elements generally covered in specifications lists are roof, walls, floors, plumbing, heating, electric wiring, insulation, doors and windows (sometimes called "fenestration"), appliances, and millwork (cabinets, closet shelves, molding, etc.).

As a rule, the specifications listed by a manufacturer are the same for all of his units, with the exception of interior finishing and trim, which varies with the "lines" offered. Deluxe models will be more elaborate than standard or economy models.

The specifications list, an exact statement about all materials and appliances, should be part and parcel of your contract with the manufacturer. You may wish to have a builder or architect take a look at the final specifications list if only to see whether substandard materials are used.

Every manufacturer also offers a list of options, which can range from better materials to more elaborate appliances or design features. In some cases, which are discussed below, it is recommended that you exercise your option for larger or better items even though they cost more.

Mobile and modular manufacturers will list, or should list, every element within the house. Prefabricated housing manufacturers will always list every element of their package, and some will recommend a certain level of quality for materials which the manufacturer does not supply but which he

139

hopes the buyer will follow so that the home will have a uniformity of quality.

The specifications given below are a distillation of the materials lists we received from all manufacturers who answered our repeated inquiries. These are listed, with addresses, in the preceding chapters. The specifications, of course, were prevalent at the time the book was written. Even though materials and construction techniques may change, the levels of quality offered by each of the types of manufactured housing probably remain the same. The prefabricated home is still of better quality than the mobile; the mobile is still cheaper than the prefabricated home; and the modular home is somewhere in between.

Before launching into the ranges of materials and comparisons among the three forms of manufactured housing, it might be useful to know just how each of these homes is fabricated, especially since various aspects of the manufacturing process affect the quality of the home.

How a Mobile Home is Built

We will here summarize the procedures of one manufacturer to explain the process. Bear in mind that exact procedures vary from manufacturer to manufacturer.

The frame consists of two I-beam steel members running from end to end and braced with welded steel cross members and outriggers. This chassis has an axle and wheels and a hitch, which is what makes the unit mobile.

The subfloor is then constructed and the heat duct (carrier of heat and air conditioning) is strapped on top of the subfloor. Water supply and drain lines are then strapped to the floor joists beside the heat duct and the insulation is rolled out over the entire length and width of the subfloor, covering ducts and water and drain lines. A layer of asphalt-impregnated all-weather board (simplex) is stapled to the edge of the floor. The frame is attached to the subfloor. Then the floor is turned over, the flooring is completely sanded and swept clean, and the linoleum and/or carpeting is rolled out, stretched, and stapled to the floor. Very ingenious indeed.

Side and end walls are next—structured, studded, windows blocked out, and insulated. Interior paneling is then attached to the interior walls. Interior partition walls are also built. The walls and partitions, by now fully insulated and paneled, are assembled into the shape of the structure.

The roof unit, the next element, will include the ceilings one sees when standing inside the mobile unit. It is a fully prepared roof and fully insulated at this point, but with a relatively shallow pitch. The structural members of the roof are wood, the exterior is metal which is then applied to the roof. With the metal now on the roof, drip rails (much smaller than gutters) are installed.

The exterior siding, for this manufacturer, is prepainted aluminum sheets which are then attached to the structure after which windows and doors are installed.

During the above steps electric lines have been put into place.

Work on the interior fixtures begins. At this point, the entire structure is complete, each room is defined, has its walls, doorway, and ceiling, has its roll goods on its subfloors, has its windows and doors in place, its roof is completed, and the entire structure is mounted on its permanent, movable chassis.

Closets are then finished, shelves installed, doors placed, and all of the decor package ordered by the customer is installed.

This is the skin and bones of the entire procedure. It sounds simple but is in fact extremely complex, requiring many individual steps of highly exact engineering and construction.

We should point out, though, that the Center for Auto Safety study of mobile housing (see the bibliography) pointed to many instances of shoddy construction within the industry, caused in part, CAS claims, by manufacturers' desire to get as many units through the assembly line per day as physically possible. Some manufacturers offer bonuses if more units than required come through the plant per day, or give the

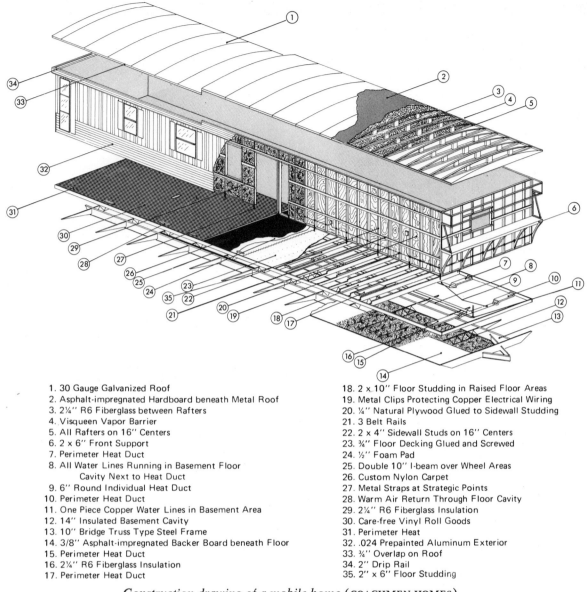

1. 30 Gauge Galvanized Roof
2. Asphalt-impregnated Hardboard beneath Metal Roof
3. 2¼" R6 Fiberglass between Rafters
4. Visqueen Vapor Barrier
5. All Rafters on 16" Centers
6. 2 x 6" Front Support
7. Perimeter Heat Duct
8. All Water Lines Running in Basement Floor Cavity Next to Heat Duct
9. 6" Round Individual Heat Duct
10. Perimeter Heat Duct
11. One Piece Copper Water Lines in Basement Area
12. 14" Insulated Basement Cavity
13. 10" Bridge Truss Type Steel Frame
14. 3/8" Asphalt-impregnated Backer Board beneath Floor
15. Perimeter Heat Duct
16. 2¼" R6 Fiberglass Insulation
17. Perimeter Heat Duct
18. 2 x 10" Floor Studding in Raised Floor Areas
19. Metal Clips Protecting Copper Electrical Wiring
20. ¼" Natural Plywood Glued to Sidewall Studding
21. 3 Belt Rails
22. 2 x 4" Sidewall Studs on 16" Centers
23. ¾" Floor Decking Glued and Screwed
24. ½" Foam Pad
25. Double 10" I-beam over Wheel Areas
26. Custom Nylon Carpet
27. Metal Straps at Strategic Points
28. Warm Air Return Through Floor Cavity
29. 2¼" R6 Fiberglass Insulation
30. Care-free Vinyl Roll Goods
31. Perimeter Heat
32. .024 Prepainted Aluminum Exterior
33. ¾" Overlap on Roof
34. 2" Drip Rail
35. 2" x 6" Floor Studding

Construction drawing of a mobile home (COACHMEN HOMES)

workers the rest of the day off when they have completed their per diem quota. Clearly, given the same crew, if quantity is the goal, quality is bound to be sacrificed. But then, how many times have you bought a new car which was delivered with all sorts of major and minor problems?

How a Modular Home is Built

Modular homes follow many of the basic procedures and steps mentioned above, with some exceptions. No chassis is constructed, for the modular is not intended to be moved once set on its foundation. Modulars take somewhat longer to construct, and they use better materials, better techniques, and provide, generally, larger amounts of space than mobiles.

How a Prefabricated Home is Built

Prefabricated homes take longer to build than either mobile or modular homes. The

A modular home plant (CONTINENTAL HOMES)

factory does little assembling; manufacturers of precut homes do virtually no assembling, manufacturers of panelized homes do more assembling. The precut wood or panels are then shipped to the site where a crew erects the home working from a construction manual supplied by the manufacturer. Prefabricated homes have the highest construction standards and use the best materials.

Roofing—Mobile Homes

The norm seems to be a one-piece sheet of galvanized steel rolled onto the roof structure. Wherever a thickness was specified it was 30 gauge. Rafters were described as truss type, spaced 16″ on center. Where weight loads were given they were 20 or 30 pounds per square foot. You should have the heaviest weight load possible if you live in an area with much snow. Some sources recommend 40 pounds per square foot for areas with extreme climatic conditions. Mobile home roofs have less of a pitch than other types of housing. The smaller the pitch, the greater the possibility of water, and certainly snow, sitting atop the roof, which is not desirable. The roof should be vented to prevent moisture problems.

Roofing—Modular Home

Roof framing is usually a series of trusses or rafters of 2 × 4s or 2 × 6s spaced 16″ on 24″ on center. Trusses are considered better than rafters as they diffuse the weight of the roof better and they are self-supporting. A rafter system requires a load-bearing wall at the center point of the ceiling joists. The less the space between rafters or trusses, the greater the weight load of the roof, which is especially critical in areas with heavy snow. Rafter wood is frequently No. 2 fir.

A word about wood. It is important to

know the kind of wood used for supporting members (floor joists, wall studs, ceiling joists, roof rafters or trusses). Different species of wood have different strengths under stress. The highest stress values are found in Douglas fir, southern yellow pine, and western larch. These are followed by cypress, redwood, and tamarack and all other softwoods take up the rear.* Woods also come in several grades, the most common of which are, from strongest to weakest, Structural, Construction, Standard, and Utility. Framing elements that support weight should be structural or construction grade, and the woods should be kiln-dried, which manufacturers should specify, so that they are less subject to shrinkage and warpage. Green wood should not be used.

* George K. Stegman and Harry J. Stegman, *Architectural Drafting: Functional Planning and Creative Design*. (Chicago: American Technical Society, 1966).

Plywood sheathing of ⅜″ or ½″ thickness is placed atop the trusses or rafters. Some manufacturers place a layer or two of felt on top of the sheathing as an underlayment for the roofing. Felt is specified by weight, usually 15 or 30 pounds.

Asphalt shingles are attached to the structure at this point. Asphalt is a better fire retardant than wood; some municipalities will not permit wood shingles or shakes. Three grades of asphalt shingles are commonly available, labeled A, B, and C. A and B include asbestos fibers for more fire retardation and are recommended. Self-sealed shingles—which have higher adherence to the siding or roof—are recommended in areas with high winds.

Manufacturers will often specify asphalt shingles by their weight in pounds. The most common range is from under 200 pounds to under 300 pounds. These figures represent the weight of a "bundle"; three "bundles"

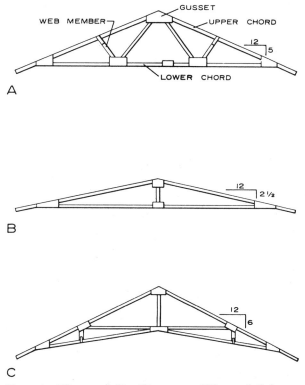

Trusses: W-type (A), King-post (B), and Scissors (C). The figures 5:12, 2½:12, and 6:12 indicate roof pitch

equal one "square"; one "square" equals 100 square feet. Needless to say, the heavier the asphalt shingles the better.

Some modular manufacturers use poor grades of felt and shingles and some do not use sheathing as a standard part of their roofs. However, the plywood sheathing may be available as an option, and it is worthwhile.

Gutters and drainspouts are not standard but are generally available as options. You might, however, choose to buy them locally and install them yourself. Installation is not difficult. Gutters collect rain water and melting snow at the edges of the roof so that the water does not drip down along the edges of the roof and splash mud along the sides of the house. Mud splashes stain the sides of the house and, over a period of time, may damage the siding. The drainspout diverts collected rain water to a suitable area. This is advisable if your land has been improperly graded so that water can accumulate in puddles along the foundation and seep into the basement.

Make sure that the attic, if you have one, is properly vented to prevent moisture problems.

Roofing—Prefabricated Homes

The pitched roof consists of either trusses or rafters attached to a ridge beam with collar ties across. Rafters are usually spaced 16″ on center, trusses 24″ on center. For a gambrel or the curved roof used by Bow House, a system of curved rafters is used.

A number of different roof styles are available from prefabricated home manufacturers. Ridge Homes will build whichever roof you want from their catalogue. Manufacturers who consider the roof to be an integral part of the design do not allow for substitutions. The most commonly offered roofs are gable (the kind of roof that most homes have), gambrel, hip, and mansard.

In a post-and-beam construction system the weight of the roof is supported by the

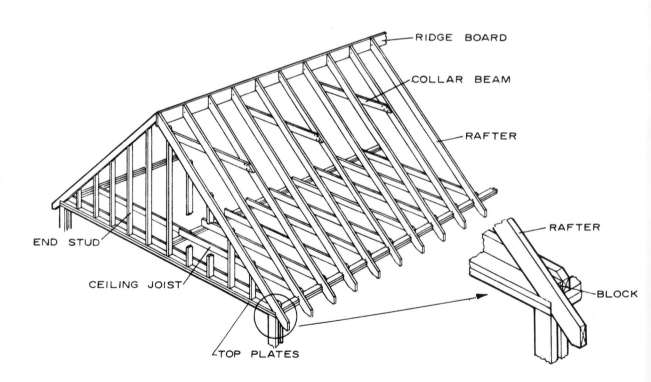

Rafter construction for gable roof

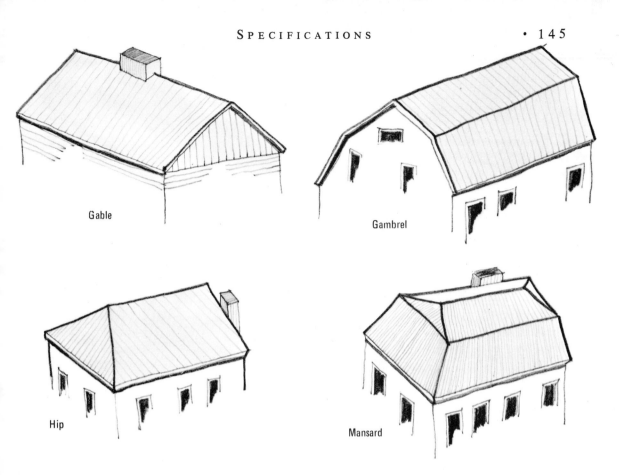

Popular roof styles: gable, gambrel, hip, and mansard

beams and no additional support, such as weight-bearing partition walls, is needed. This permits the dramatic interiors with cathedral ceilings that are found in the homes built by Acorn, Deck House, Lindal, Tech-built, and others.

Several manufacturers offer a natural wood tongue-in-groove planking or decking for their roofs, such as 3 × 8 cedar, 2 × 6 rough-sawn cedar, and pine. The ceiling that you see from inside forms the sheathing upon which is placed the insulation, felt, and shingles. The natural wood ceiling inside the home creates a warm feeling.

In a system which is not planking or decking, a layer of plywood sheathing, usually between ⅜″ and ½″, is attached to the trusses or rafters. A layer of felt, usually of 15 pound weight, is applied. Asphalt shingles (most manufacturers use 235-pound shingles, some go as high as 290 pound shingles)

is then attached. Several manufacturers offer cedar shakes and shingles as options. Other forms of roofing, such as terra cotta tile or slate, are rarely available because of their high cost (they are expensive to buy and are especially expensive to transport because of their weight).

A word about shingles and shakes. They are both pretty much the same, one difference being in size and thickness. Shingles are smaller than shakes. Cedar is the most common material, though other woods are also used. Three grades are generally available, called first, second, and third grade, with first grade being the best. The advantage of shingles and shakes is that the natural wood has a resistance to decay, which means little if any maintenance. The wood can be easily stained for a long-lasting appearance. If the wood is kept in its natural form, with no finish applied, it will color,

Post-and-beam construction (AMERICAN BARN)

turning to a beautiful gray with time. Shakes, by the way, are also frequently used as siding as well as roofing. Shingles are generally factory-made; shakes are hand cut and are more weather resistant.

Roofing—Domes

The "roof" of the dome is also its wall. Most often each of the triangles that make up the dome structure is made of the same material, usually ½″-thick plywood paneling, which is treated for exterior use (called exterior grade or marine grade plywood) and attached to a frame of Douglas fir 2 × 4s. The braces, when specified, are also Douglas fir 2 × 4s. The manufacturers of domes who responded to our queries did not specify the grade of the Douglas fir.

Walls—Mobile Homes

Exterior siding on mobile homes is almost always aluminum of a generally unspecified gauge. The two manufacturers who did so, specified .024 gauge aluminum. At least two companies, Dickman Homes and Lakewood Industries, offer wood siding. Interior walls are usually ¼″ plywood panels attached to studs. Some manufacturers offer other types of finished wall as options. The paneling is mounted on 2 × 3 studs placed

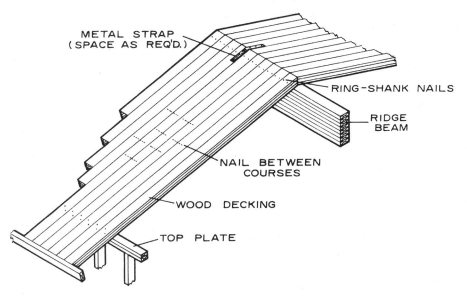

Roof decking with ridge beam

16″ on center, though several companies offer 2 × 4 studs or what they call "3″ walls," which we read as 2 × 3s. Many wall systems use crosspieces (belt rails) as well. Insulation, which is discussed later, is placed between the paneling and exterior siding.

Walls—Modular Homes

Wall framing is nearly always 2 × 4 studs spaced 16″ on center. Some specifications lists give additional wall construction details, such as sill plate size, headers over windows, and bridging between studs. If these are not mentioned in the specifications lists, do not assume that they do not exist. Ask about them. A few modular manufacturers use 2 × 3 studs for interior walls, but this might prevent these units from complying with many building codes. Those manufacturers offering 2 × 3s as standard may also offer 2 × 4s as an option.

Interior walls are drywall (also known as gypsum, sheetrock, or wallboard) either ⅜″ or ½″ thick, or ¼″ wood paneling attached directly to the studs, or a combination of the two. The ¼″ paneling is cheaper than drywall, but some consider it a fire hazard, and paneling does little as a sound deadener.

Exterior siding is usually aluminum, fiberboard, or rough-sawn plywood made to look like wood siding—e.g. clapboard, board and batten. Some manufacturers offer plywood sheathing behind the siding as standard; others offer it as an option. Modular manufacturers frequently identify the brand names of the siding used (Masonite, Georgia Pacific, Humboldt, etc.), but do not mention the thickness of the siding.

Walls—Prefabricated Homes

The structural system used for the walls will define the "look" of the home and the flexibility of its floor plan. Several systems are used by the industry. One is the conventional framing system (also followed by the mobile and modular manufacturers). Conventional prefabricated framing consists of vertical studs, usually 2 × 4s spaced 16″ on center, with reinforced studs (2 × 4s doubled or tripled) at window and door openings and at corners.

The exterior wall is formed by nailing sheathing to the studs, with the siding nailed

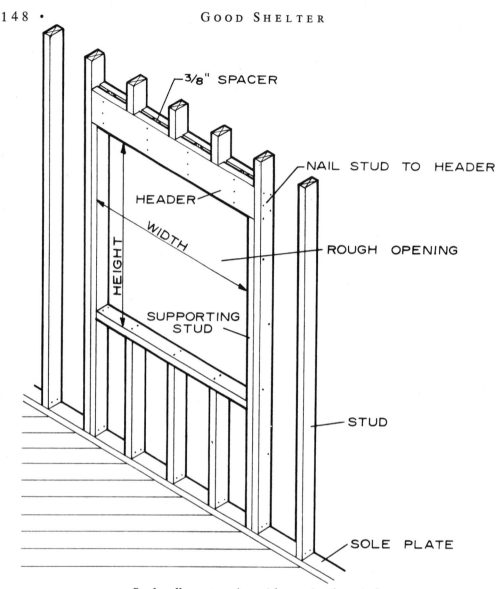

Stud wall construction with opening for window

to the sheathing. A wide variety of materials are used. The interior walls are formed by nailing the interior paneling, usually ½" sheetrock, to the studs. Bow House uses a plaster-type finishing as it attempts to reproduce an early New England home of a time which predates wallboard. Insulation is placed between the sheathing and the sheetrock.

A second type of wall system is post-and-beam construction. Because the posts and beams carry the weight of the roof, none of the walls are load-bearing and, consequently, can be built with virtually any material—glass, screens, or conventional stud framing with siding and sheating for the exterior and sheetrock for the interior. The interior walls can be anywhere and in any shape you wish. One manufacturer, Flexi-Panel, offers a "sandwich" panel of 1½"-thick particle board with ⅛" Masonite panels attached to both sides. Flexi-Panel claims that these wall materials form a natural insulation. Clearly, the use of this "sandwich" panel eliminates the extra labor involved in installing siding and interior finish wall.

A third system is the "log cabin" wall of

thick, log-like wooden pieces stacked one on top of the other and notched so that each log fits tightly on the one below. Natural wood forms the exterior and interior walls; no sheathing, siding, or sheetrock is needed. And because of its thickness, it is its own insulation, assuming there are no air spaces between logs. One manufacturer, Pan-Abode, offers logs for the interior partition walls for a total rustic look.

How, you might ask, does one hide electric wiring and plumbing lines in a structure like a log cabin which has no space between the interior and exterior walls? The answer is a special groove at the base of the log wall in which the electrician runs his wire, and the groove is then covered so it will not be noticed. The wall that contains the plumbing lines is covered with wallboard.

These three systems deal with vertical walls. But what about those homes whose walls do not rise at a 90° angle, such as A-frames, geodesic domes, and the fascinating Hexaplex described in the prefabricated housing chapter?

Viewed from the front, an A-frame is triangular in shape. Its walls are formed by its roof. Prefabricated A-frames are constructed

Notched log cabin wall (VERMONT LOG BUILDINGS)

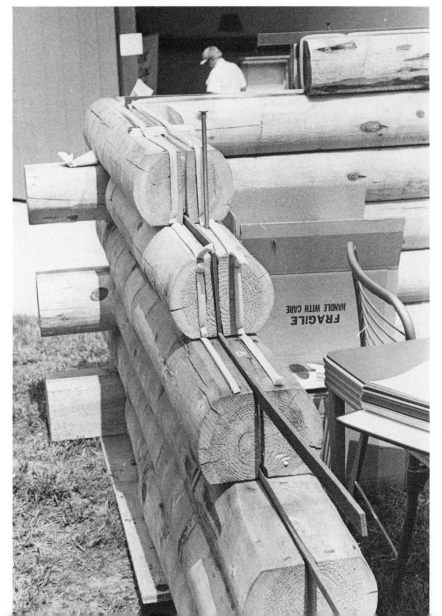

by some manufacturers following the post and beam system, while others use a conventional stud wall system.

The Hexaplex home, like the geodesic dome, has walls which form the roof and which are self-supporting.

An outer covering is needed on the exterior. These coverings usually are ½" plywood layers, then a layer of felt or other protective covering, then the actual siding. Hardboard siding or aluminum laid horizontally provides a traditional look. Aluminum seen up close always looks like aluminum, no matter what it is supposed to simulate. If you really want wood, get it even though it might cost more. Horizontal siding gives a clapboard effect. A more modern effect would be created with a plywood having a textured surface to look like natural wood— rough-sawn plywood is an example—or actual boards or shakes of cedar or redwood. The initial cost of redwood or cedar is greater than other forms of siding. Redwood and cedar have natural keeping properties and require virtually no upkeep; if pine is used for the exteriors, it must be treated with preservatives periodically. And please remember that natural woods which are not painted or stained will change color as they weather.

Insulation

This is the very important factor that insures that the house can maintain a comfortable temperature and will be reasonably economical to heat. Fiberglass is the most widely used insulant in manufactured housing. All manufacturers specify the amount of fiberglass used in one of two ways: by thickness in inches or by an R rating.

The "R" stands for "resistance to heat flow" and is a performance standard rather than a material rating. One should not be overly concerned with the type of materials used as long as the necessary R rating is met and the materials are not flammable. An R rating is a better criterion than inches of fiberglass, for this material is available in a number of grades, which manufacturers do not specify.

The thickness of the fiberglass is not as important as the number of air spaces per square inch, for it is the air space and not the material which is the insulant. A thick piece of fiberglass with fewer air spaces may not work as well as a thin piece with many spaces.

Obviously, the colder the climate the higher the R rating should be. The higher the R rating the more warm air kept inside the home in winter and the more cool air kept inside in summer. Most manufacturers will provide additional insulation as an option, and we suggest that you take it.

Here is one suggested R rating table*, with insulation also given in the rough equivalent in inches of fiberglass.

Ceiling insulation: R-19 for cold climate or homes with electric heat; requires 5" to 7" of fiberglass. R-13 (3" to 4" of fiberglass) is

* The high-lows are based on our review of manufacturers specifications lists. The R rating and inch equivalent is from A. M. Watkins, *Building or Buying the Highest Quality House at the Lowest Cost* (Garden City, N.Y.: Doubleday, 1962).

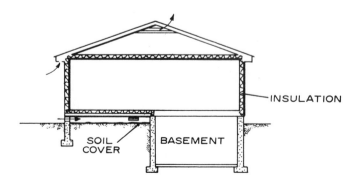

Placement of insulation

adequate for homes heated by other means. Manufacturers' specifications ranged between 1⅛″ and 7″. Units with minimal insulation may be marketed in warm climate areas.

Wall insulation: R-11 for cold climate or homes with electric heat; requires 2½″ to 3″ of fiberglass. R-8 (1½″ to 2½″ of fiberglass) is adequate for homes heated by other means. Manufacturers' specifications ranged between 1¼″ and 4″. Units with minimal insulation may be marketed in warm climate areas.

Floor insulation: R-13 for cold climate or homes with electric heat; requires 2″ to 3″ of fiberglass. R-9 (1½″ to 2½″ of fiberglass) is adequate for homes heated by other means. Manufacturers' specifications ranged between 1⅛″ and 6″. Units with minimal insulation may be marketed in warm climate areas.

As many manufacturers do not specify R ratings but virtually always specify inches of fiberglass, here is a comparison of the range found in each type of house in inches:

Ceiling insulation:
Mobiles—1⅛″ to 6½″
Modulars—3″ to 7″
Prefabricated—2¼″ to 6″
Wall insulation:
Mobiles—1¼″ to 3¼″
Modulars—2″ to 4″
Prefabricated—2¼″ to 3⅝″
Floor insulation:
Mobiles—1⅛″ to 3¼″
Modulars—2″ to 6″
Prefabricated—2″ to 6″

A few prefabricated housing manufacturers do not use fiberglass. Manufacturers producing a decking or planking roofing system, where the insulation is on the outside, use a dense, rigid insulant on top of the roof, under the shingles. Some dome manufacturers also use a rigid insulant or a foam. The most common names for these insulants are urethane and celotex.

The manufacturers of prefabricated log cabins claim that the thickness of the wood is a natural insulant, and they use no insulation whatsoever in the walls.

Floors—Mobiles

Flooring consists of insulation, joists, a layer of subflooring, and linoleum, sheet vinyl, or carpeting above the subfloor. Carpeting is usually used throughout the house with the exception of the kitchen and bathroom, which have linoleum or vinyl floors. Some inexpensive models may have more vinyl than carpeting. The quality of the carpeting, and the use of a pad—"underlayment"—between the subfloor and the carpet, will depend on the overall cost of the unit. Deluxe units will have plusher carpeting than economy models.

Joists were usually 2 × 6s spaced 16″ on center, but one manufacturer used 2 × 5s and another used 2 × 4s. The 2 × 6 joists are best and are less likely to cause sagging floors.

Subflooring was invariably ⅝″-thick particle board (also called composition board) or fir plywood. Where other homes would have a foundation, mobiles have their chassis, usually 10″ or 12″ I-beams of steel, the thickness of the beam depending upon the width and length of the home.

Floors—Modulars

Floor framing consists of 2 × 6 or 2 × 8 joists spaced 16″ on center. Sometimes other parts of the floor framing will also be described in specifications lists, such as the perimeter plate (also called rim joist, frame, perimeter boxing, or box sill), girders, and bridging. According to one source, cross bridging between joists is advisable, for it will help prevent squeaking floors. Others disagree. The best way to prevent floor squeaking is to have the wood flooring nailed very securely to the subfloor. Noisy floors probably do not strike you as critical, at this point; just try living with them. But all agree that bridging helps to prevent sagging floors. Cross bridging should be in rows of 1 × 3 braces between the joists, with the rows spaced a maximum of 8′ apart.

Upon these joists is the subfloor, which is plywood sheets ranging between ½″ to 1″ thick, with ⅝″ the norm. Attached to the subfloor is either carpeting, vinyl tile, sheet vinyl, vinyl asbestos tile, and, very occasionally, ceramic tile and hardwood floors. Hopefully, the manufacturers you contact will specify the thicknesses of the flooring materials they use, as the range of quality is great.

Floors—Prefabricated

A floor framing system and subfloor is almost always included in a prefabricated home package. The underpinning of the floor is a series of girder beams whose thickness depends upon the distance to be spanned and the weight to be supported. A two-story home, for instance, is heavier than a one-story home and requires larger girders. Common girder sizes are 4 × 10, 6 × 10, 2 × 12 doubled, and 6 × 8 tripled. The floor framing members set on the girders are called joists and they are either 2 × 8s or 2 × 10s usually spaced 16″ on center. If the house has an attic or second floor, ceiling joists are needed to support the upper floor, but they need not be as strong as those which support the weight of the lower floor. Ceiling joists usually are 2 × 6s.

If the floor framing system has bridging, it is identical to the specifications of modular homes.

An alternate flooring system, used by Deck House among others, consists of 3 × 8 cedar decking nailed directly to 4 × 12 beams serving as girders. This decking is the frame, subfloor, and finish floor all in one, as well as the ceiling for the floor below. The company claims the floor is so strong you "can drive a truck on it." In a standard flooring system there is space between the subfloor of the upper story and the ceiling of the lower story for hiding electric wiring and ducts for heating or air conditioning, but a deck system has no such space. Hot air heating systems would be difficult to install

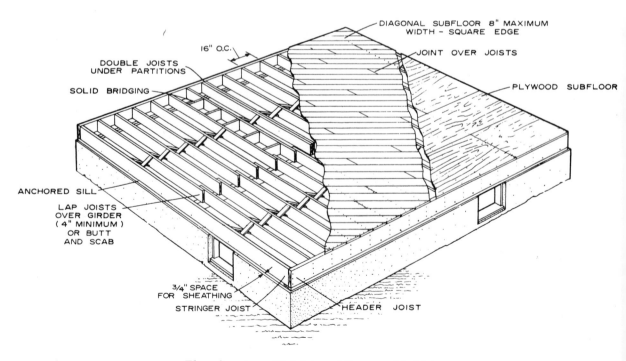

Floor framing with joists, subfloor, and bridging

in a home with deck ceilings, and hanging light fixtures may pose difficult, but not insoluble, problems.

Attached to the joists, in buildings not using a decking system, is a subflooring of plywood, usually between $\frac{5}{16}''$ and $\frac{3}{4}''$ thick, with the most common thicknesses being $\frac{1}{2}''$ and $\frac{5}{8}''$. Atop this is the finish flooring—wood, carpet, vinyl, linoleum, quarry tile—which is usually not provided in the manufacturer's package.

Electric Wiring

Wiring should be adequate to support a full range of typical appliances, the heating system, and whatever high-powered equipment you might be using, say, in a workshop. Electric baseboard heating requires a 200-ampere service, and many all-electric homes provide this power. The range of amperage goes from 50 to 200 amperes, with mobiles on the low end and the modulars and prefabricated homes usually providing the maximum needed for the type of heating used.

When you consider your power needs, remember that electrical power consists of volts and amperes which, when multiplied, yield watts. The higher the wattage, the greater the number of electrical devices that can be used simultaneously.

Here's an idea of what uses how much wattage. One source* indicates that a clothes dryer may use between 4500 and 9000 watts or, in terms of your electric bill, 4½ to 9 kilowatt hours for each hour of use, and is the biggest electricity-consuming appliance in a home. An electric broiler can go as high as 1800 or more watts (1.8 kilowatt hours per 1 hour of service). Those electric appliances that create heat have higher wattages than those that do not. A refrigerator is rated at 150 watts, a television at 250 watts, a radio at 30 watts, a coffee maker at 1000 watts, an electric skillet at 1100 watts, an electric hot plate at 1650

* Robert Schwartz and Hubbard H. Cobb, *The Complete Homeowner* (New York: Macmillan, 1965), p. 224.

watts, a dishwasher at 1300 watts, a clothes washer at 400 watts. Add to this the wattage needed to run the heating system and an electric stove, and you'll have a good idea of how much wattage you may need.

A word about electric wire. Copper is still the best conductor. A number of mobile manufacturers installed aluminum wire. Aluminum is also an excellent conductor but it cannot be bent as well as copper to make connections to outlet boxes. When aluminum wire was used, it had a tendency to break, causing shorts and fires. Stay away from aluminum wire if you can. Your chances of coming across aluminum wiring in a new mobile are slight. The reverse may be true if you plan buying a used mobile home.

Mobile home manufacturers are unusually reticent about their electrical wiring. Just about the only information you can get out of them, if you're lucky, is the amperage count. However, if you are in a buying situation rather than just looking, chances are good that you will get all of the information you need.

Modular manufacturers give more information and also tend to have options for circuit breakers, which are very useful and which some mobile manufacturers do not offer.

Electrical wiring may not be provided by the prefabricated home manufacturer, if only because it would have to be installed on the site, and you might do much better with a local electrician who knows local requirements and who can read the manufacturer's construction manual. Electrical wiring is easily installed in a prefabricated home, so you should have no problems whatsoever. But plan in advance, establish which appliances you intend to install and where you plan to place them. It is probably a good idea to plan for just about every kind of appliance, even though you may never buy all of them. It is inexpensive to have the electrician wire for these appliances while the walls are unfinished, and very expensive to go into finished walls at some later date. Remember, even though you might not require some appliances, it is possible that when you have to sell your home the buyer would be interested in all of the special wiring and outlets.

Heating

The most common heating systems within the mobile and modular housing industries are electric baseboard heat and gas-fired hot air heat. Only one manufacturer offers oil-fired hot water. Most manufacturers of prefabricated homes do not offer heating systems, but prefer the buyer to make his selection and have the system installed on the site by local labor.

Both electric baseboard heating and hot air are inexpensive systems to install, operate well, and heat a home quickly. Electric baseboard is the cheapest heating system to install, requiring only wiring and the attachment of inexpensive baseboard units. Hot air heating is more expensive for the manufacturer, as it requires a furnace and duct work to draw cold air into the furnace, heat it, and send hot air out through the ducts. The advantage of hot air is that it can easily be converted to an air conditioning system. A disadvantage is that the furnace requires maintenance and repair. Electric baseboard heat's overwhelming advantage is that many thermostats can be installed throughout the house so that one can easily control temperatures throughout the structure. This is especially valuable in winter, when rooms not in use can be entirely shut off. Hot air heat can have several heating "zones," but the more zones the more expensive to install the system, and no matter how many zones are built into a home, they will never equal the "fine tuning" available from electric baseboard heat. If you choose a zoned hot air system, you must make your wishes known to the manufacturer before work is begun on your unit. It is prohibitively expensive to decide to add additional zones after the house has been completed. Supporters of hot water systems claim that this form of heating provides the most even heat and the heated air is moist, not as dry as hot air or electric baseboard heat. But it is the most expensive to install, is noisy

and slow, and strikes us as having more potential malfunctions than the other forms of heating.

On the whole, if a manufacturer offers hot air as standard, take it, even though the fuel used to fire the system is rapidly increasing in price and may be in short supply. In some parts of the country local gas companies are not accepting new customers. Electricity, too, is rising in cost, but there are parts of the country where electricity is a bargain, and other parts where it is very expensive. Regardless of the heating system, be sure you have more than adequate insulation.

Let us digress for a moment. For years we have heard that electric heat is more expensive than oil. Yet, for us, electric heating has proved to be somewhat less expensive than oil-fired hot water. Our geodesic domes are heated by electric baseboards; the old farmhouse we previously owned was heated by hot water radiators.

Here's a method for calculating the form of home heating—oil or electricity—which would be most economical, given to us by one of the country's leading mechanical engineers.

After going through a complex series of calculations based on BTUs (British Thermal Units) produced and heat losses, he came to the conclusion that where one gallon of fuel oil costs less than 15 kilowatt hours of electricity, use oil; where one gallon of oil costs more than 15 kilowatt hours of electricity, use electricity. When you ask your electric company for the cost per kilowatt hour make sure of two things—that the quoted price includes the fuel adjustment charge and that it is based on your anticipated use of electricity (as strange as it might seem in these days of energy crises, the more electricity you use the lower the rate per kilowatt hour).

When you are making your decision it will be based on prevailing costs, which may fluctuate. As oil is the primary fuel for electricity generating plants, costs will depend in large measure upon whether oil is in plentiful or scarce supply. This factor will also affect the user of oil in a home furnace.

But electricity can be generated by means other than oil, such as water power, nuclear power, and coal. Coal, which is a fossil fuel in abundant supply in the United States, is used only by some electric generating plants, though their number is increasing. So ask yourself where you think your electricity will come from in the future—will it still come from fossil fuels or will other means, which might be less expensive, be used. A crystal ball or ouija board will help.

To further compound the issue, here is a moral point to ponder. The home owner with an oil burning furnace, believe it or not, gets more BTUs per gallon of oil than the electricity generating plant can send to its users from the same gallon of oil. So, on a gallon per gallon basis, the individual home furnace uses less oil than the electricity user for the same amount of heat. But the electric companies, buying oil in such vast quantities, effect a cost savings per gallon of oil which the individual home owner cannot hope to approach. Users of power generated by hydroelectricity have the best of both worlds—lower cost and they do not use fossil fuels.

Where we live, the costs for electricity and oil heat are roughly equivalent. Other parts of the country may have a significant difference between the two. For example, the Federal Power Commission's report on all-electric homes in the United States,* which analyzed annual electric bills as of January 1, 1970 in cities of 50,000 or more, showed that the rate for each kilowatt hour of power ranged from 0.79¢ (Seattle) to 2.81¢ (Hilo, Hawaii) on the basis of 15,000 kilowatts usage per annum and from 0.78¢ (Seattle) to 2.48¢ (Hilo) on the basis of 30,000 kilowatt hours. That is a difference of more than 350% for the same hour of power at 15,000 kilowatts and close to 320% at 30,000 kilowatts.

A recommended hot-air system furnace size for homes in cold climates is 40 to 55 BTUs per square foot of living area. Or, as a

concrete example, a 24′ × 44′ (1056 square feet) home should have a furnace capability of at least 45,000 BTUs.

Only two mobile home manufacturers gave the BTU rating of their furnaces (65,000 and 72,000 BTUs), which were more than adequate for the models in which the furnaces were placed. A small number of modular home manufacturers gave BTU ratings, and those listed ranged from 82,000 to 110,000 BTUs, also more than adequate. We think it very important for you to know the capacity of the furnace in BTUs and to ascertain whether the standard furnace will be adequate for your needs. We don't think you will appreciate being cold in your home in the dead of winter with your furnace going full blast.

Plumbing

No matter what kind of manufactured home you buy, you will need a plumber. The mobile home buyer who is placing his unit on his own land will need a plumber (who might be provided by the dealer) to do all of the rough plumbing prior to the arrival of the mobile home and to make the connections to the well or public water supply and to the septic system or public sewerage. The same is true for the modular home owner. The prefabricated home owner needs a plumber to do all interior plumbing as well as the rough plumbing and hookups.

For some reason which escapes us you have to watch the plumber every second. Some frequently forget to read specifications or have a low opinion of the prevailing plumbing codes and go their merry way. We don't know why plumbers—and we are generalizing—do, or rather, don't do these things, but they apparently require more supervision than masons, electricians, carpenters, or even excavators.

In our case, we specified plastic pipes for sewage lines because the materials are cheaper than copper or cast iron and because installation is faster. The plumber forgot to read the specifications and installed all copper plumbing. That was his loss. However,

* Federal Power Commission, Bureau of Power. *All Electric Homes in the United States: Annual Bills—January 1, 1970, Cities of 50,000 and More* (Washington, D.C.: U.S. Government Printing Office).

as soon as he realized his error, he tried to skimp on labor and materials elsewhere.

How can plumbers cheat a little here or there? You specify ½″ pipe, they install ⅜″ pipe; you specify one grade, they install a cheaper grade.

During the entire construction of our home, we fought only with the plumber. When the contractor took the side of the plumber, we fought with the contractor. The kitchen sink vent was improperly installed, frost-free sillcocks (fancy term for outdoor faucets) were not frost free, and some of the plumbing lines had to be replaced with larger pipes. The plumber did not want to correct any of these errors, some of which violated the state's plumbing code, but we did not pay him until he made good, which he eventually did. We lost two weeks as a result, but our contract had a penalty clause in it and the builder had to deduct the penalty from his final amount due.

Here is the clincher. We wanted the plumber to take an air pressure test, which many local building codes and state plumbing codes require. An air pressure test will show if there are any leaks in the plumbing before water is introduced into the lines and causes damage. He refused. All work on our home stopped. Finally, he agreed to make the test.

Air tests are simple. You close the entire system, bring in a small compressor, pump air into the system to a given pressure, stick on a pressure gauge and wait and see if the needle drops appreciably. If it does you have a leak, if it doesn't the system is fine. Ten pounds per square inch loss in an hour's time isn't bad.

On the test day the system was sealed, an aged compressor was attached, and we finally got the pressure up, but not to the point required by the state code. On went the gauge. The needle dropped like a lead balloon. The system wasn't properly sealed, said the plumber, so we'll try again in a few days.

We asked a builder friend, who, it turned out, went to high school with the plumber, to witness the second try. Along came the plumber with his compressor. It chugged and pumped away but could just barely produce a pressure equal to about half the pressure specified by the codes. The plumber shrugged his shoulders, smiled sheepishly, and said that he could do no more. It was just like a Hollywood movie of rural America. Our friend calmly walked to his car and brought out a spanking new compressor. We attached the compressor and brought the pressure up to the state requirements. And after all of this delay, argument, and stubbornness, the system was good.

Mobile home manufacturers describe their plumbing systems in very sketchy terms. You may learn the capacity of the water heater (range was from 17 to 40 gallons with quick recovery heaters offered as options); you may learn that the pipes are copper, galvanized steel, or plastic; but you won't learn the diameter of the pipes, the horsepower of the water pump, and so on.

Modular home manufacturers offer more help. Water pipes are usually ½″ copper and one manufacturer offers a ¾″ feed line and ½″ runs. Drain pipes, which carry used water and sewage, are usually plastic, referred to as PVC (polyvinyl chloride) or ABS (acrylonitrile butadiene styrene), between 1½″ and 3″ in diameter. One company specified all plastic pipes except for those homes where local codes require copper. Plastic pipes are excellent for drainage; copper is advisable for water lines.

A recommended water heater for a family of three (with a washing machine) is 30 gallons if the heater is gas fired and 66 gallons if electric without a washing machine and 80 gallons with one. Gas heats water faster than electricity. Many specifications of modular home manufacturers indicated the heater's water capacity but did not indicate whether gas fired or electric or whether they were "quick recovery" systems—heaters which heat the water faster. The range was from 30 to 52 gallons, leading us to assume that they are gas fired, but this should be checked.

As for water pumps, most manufacturers offer ½-horsepower pumps as standard. A ¾-horsepower pump may be offered as an option, and it is one we advise you to take, despite the added expense, for the more powerful pump will not be strained as much as it supplies your needs.

And we suggest that you make your septic bed larger than the minimum specified in the local building codes and that you install a larger than required septic tank, if only as a precaution. We suggest that you drill deep for your well, going even deeper than the water table, if only to allow for the rising and falling of the table. It is much cheaper to anticipate a problem at the outset than to be faced by a problem later on and have to redo what had been done before.

Everything Else

Here is a grab bag of items that are usually included in the manufactured home. Many are small items that contribute to the finished look of the residence. Though the manufacturer's promotional literature may not mention them all by name, the specifications list should state each item and give an accurate description by type, size (width and depth), and thickness.

Stairs consist of stringers, treads, risers (if the steps are closed—outdoor or basement steps may be open and would not have risers), stringers, and possibly a railing. Treads should be of hardwoods, such as oak, as they probably receive more wear and tear than floors.

Windows and doors usually come from the factory prehung and are then installed in the prefabricated home; they are factory installed in modular and mobile homes. Their style and materials should reflect the overall style of the home. The window frames are generally of wood, aluminum, or vinyl-clad wood. Sizes may vary, and you may have the option of ordering larger windows.

If you live in a cold winter climate and are planning on storm windows, single-pane windows will be fine. If you are planning on large picture windows or glass walls, where storm windows are impossible to find, we strongly recommend using insulated or vacuum sealed glass for the large areas. This form of glass is more costly at the outset but will definitely save money when it comes to winter heating and will also prevent annoying and possibly costly condensation.

Fake shutters are available for show. A variety of exterior doors, in different styles, are usually offered. These doors are usually solid, about 1¾″ thick and 36″ or more wide. Some of these doors may have a plastic or metal covering.

Interior doors are usually hollow core, about 1⅜″ thick. Most manufacturers offer but one kind of interior door.

Don't forget to weatherstrip doors and windows before the onset of winter. Be very careful if you are weatherstripping in the area where your furnace is located. Don't make the room weathertight, for the furnace needs some fresh air and ventilation. If the weatherstripping is too tight, it may cause the flame to go out.

Other interior trim that should be specified includes baseboards and wainscot or chair rail in those models which strive to reproduce early American homes (these details would be found only in a few select prefabricated homes). You will also want to know about the cabinetry, closets, the counters in the kitchen, and all fixtures (sinks, toilets, lights, etc.).

And lastly, you will want to investigate all exterior details, such as projecting and protective roof pieces (soffits, fascias, and cornices, for example). Decks, balconies, and exterior steps are often offered by manufacturers, and you will certainly need exterior steps to get into your home. One manufacturer of prefabricated homes, Universal, goes so far as to offer fences and light posts as an option.

Compare the specifications of different manufacturers and their construction systems and costs. Don't forget to check local building codes. Make sure the manufacturer has received FHA or VA approval if you'll be applying for financial assistance from these agencies. Check the national building code organizations (BOCA, ICBO, etc.) that the manufacturer belongs to. If you are planning to do some of the work on your home yourself, make sure in advance that the local regulations will permit it.

Here is a checklist of the most common components of homes as they are built in the United States today. There are three major parts to a house: foundation, frame, and mechanical systems (heating, water supply and plumbing, electrical).

All are included in a mobile home, with the I-beam chassis serving as a built-in foundation, though the house must also rest on a prepared surface. The modular manufacturer supplies everything other than the foundation, which is built on the site. Prefabricated (panelized or precut) housing may include everything other than the foundation in the manufacturer's price quotation. However, many prefabricated home manufacturers sell only the constructed frame (interior and exterior) and let a local builder supply the mechanical systems (often to the manufacturer's specifications) and sometimes the interior finishing as well.

For each item in this list there will be various details that should help you evaluate the quality of the manufacturer's specifications. One detail is the material used: concrete, wood, brick, etc., and if wood, the kind and grade. Another detail is size, expressed as dimension for three-dimensional materials such as boards, concrete blocks, etc., as thickness for materials which are essentially two-dimensional, such as plywood, felt (usually expressed in pounds rather than thickness), siding, shingles (usually expressed in pounds), insulation, etc.; as diameter for pipes and electric wiring; or as capacity for certain appliances (refrigerators in cubic feet; clothes washers in pounds per load; water heaters in gallons; furnaces in BTUs). Another detail of value is the brand name, if only as a personal measure of the quality of the item. Some of the items identified by brand can be checked in consumer publications. If you have a problem with the item that the housing manufacturer will not or cannot resolve, you would have a second line of defense by going to the unit's manufacturer. Other items listed here are self-explanatory.

Bear in mind that when you read manu-

facturers' literature, you may not find some of the items listed here in their specifications listing. If it's not there, ask; the more information you can get, the better.

Not all manufactured housing contains all of the items listed below. For example, the number of layers of materials used for walls or flooring will vary depending upon the cost of the house. Exterior walls of an expensive unit may include plywood sheathing over the frame, plus a layer of felt, and shingles, or other siding material. A less expensive home may omit the felt, and a very inexpensive home may have the siding attached directly to the framing. This is the kind of information that will tell you why one unit costs more or less than another.

We have tried to make this list as comprehensive as possible so that you can compare different units of the same type and also compare the various kinds of manufactured housing. Your answer to the questions given below should show which manufacturers offer homes you would like to live in at the best value per dollar and at a price which you can afford. Even if you decide to build a stick-built home, this list will help you calculate costs and value:

Foundation

1. Footing (depth and width) _____
2. Foundation wall material _____ thickness _____
or Piers material _____ thickness _____
or Supporting frame material _____ thickness _____
3. Crawl space dimension _____
or Basement floor material _____ thickness _____
waterproofing _____
or Slab thickness _____
4. Termite protection _____
5. Waterproofing protection _____

Flooring

1. Framing girders material _____

Laminate (built-up)? Solid? dimension _____ spacing _____

Joists material _____ dimension _____ spacing _____

Bridging material _____ dimension _____ spacing _____

2. Subfloor material _____ thickness _____

3. Finish floor:

Living room underlayment material _____ thickness _____

Living room finish floor material _____ thickness _____

Bedroom underlayment material _____ thickness _____

Bedroom finish floor material _____ thickness _____

Kitchen underlayment material _____ thickness _____

Kitchen finish floor material _____ thickness _____

Bathroom underlayment material _____ thickness _____

Bathroom finish floor material _____ thickness _____

Other rooms underlayment material _____ thickness _____

Other rooms finish floor material _____ thickness _____

4. Insulation under ground floor material _____ thickness _____ brand name _____ R-rating _____

Exterior Walls

1. Framing: Studs material _____ dimension _____ spacing _____

Other framing details: Headers? Sills? Corner Posts? Bracing? Other?

Posts (if post-and-beam construction) material _____ dimensions _____ spacing _____

2. Sheathing material _____ thickness _____

Overlay on sheathing material _____ thickness _____

3. Siding material _____ thickness _____ overlap _____ brand name _____

4. Insulation brand name _____ ma-terial _____ thickness _____ R-rating _____

5. Other type of wall construction (describe) _____

Interior Walls

Wall framing may be the same as exterior walls; however, if walls are non-load-bearing they may be built to lesser specifications without detriment to the structure.

1. Studs material _____ dimension _____ spacing _____

Other framing details: Headers? Sills? Corner Posts? Bracing? Other?

2. Interior finish material _____ thickness _____ finish coat _____

3. Ceiling finish (may be the same as wall finish) material _____ thickness _____ finish coat _____

4. Insulation material _____ thickness _____ brand name _____ R-rating _____

5. Soundproofing material, if any _____ thickness _____

Roof

1. Roof framing rafters material _____ dimension _____ spacing _____ ridge board material _____ dimension _____

or

Truss type _____ material _____ dimension _____ spacing _____

or

Beams (if post-and-beam construction) material _____ dimension _____ spacing _____

2. Soffit?

3. Fascia?

4. Gutters or drip edge?

5. Downspout?

6. Roof vents: Ridge? Eaves? Gable?

7. Other roof construction details (describe) _____

8. Subroofing (sheathing) material _____ thickness _____

9. Underlayment material _____ weight _____ number of layers _____

10. Roofing material _____ brand name _____ weight/thickness _____ overlap, if any _____

11. Under roof insulation material _____ thickness _____ R-rating _____ brand name _____

Windows

1. Living room size _____ bedroom sizes _____ Bathroom size _____ Kitchen size _____ Other rooms sizes _____

2. Single hung? Double hung? Casement? Awning? Fixed glass? Other _____

3. Frame material _____ thickness _____

4. Single-strength glass? Double-strength glass?

5. Insulated glass? Vacuum sealed? Single-pane? Shatter-proof? Storm windows? Storm doors? Screens? Brand name? _____

Doors

1. Exterior door material _____ dimension _____ design _____

2. Door frame material _____ thickness _____

3. Interior door material _____ dimension _____

4. Closet door material _____ dimension _____ sliding doors _____

5. Exterior glass sliding door size _____ frame material _____ Type of glass: Single pane? Insulated? Vacuum sealed? Brand name? _____

Stairs

Specifications may differ for stairs leading from the first story to the second and stairs leading to the basement.

1. Tread material _____ dimension _____

2. Riser material _____ dimension _____

3. Stringer material _____ dimension _____

4. Railing material _____ dimension _____

5. Landing material _____ dimension _____

Other Interior Trim (millwork)

1. Kitchen cabinet material _____ number of cubic or linear feet _____ brand name _____

2. Kitchen counter covering material _____

3. Baseboard material _____ dimension _____

4. Molding material _____ dimension _____

Balconies, Decks, etc.

In many cases these elements are supplied by the home buyer. They may not be included in the unit cost and may not be included as options.

1. Decking material _____ dimension _____

2. Railing material _____ dimension _____

3. Exterior step material _____ dimension _____

4. Balcony material _____ dimension _____

5. Balcony railing material _____ dimension _____

Plumbing

1. Drain pipe material _____ diameter(s) _____

2. Water supply pipe material _____ diameter(s) _____

3. Plumbing supplied for clothes washer? Dishwasher?

4. Hot water heater type _____ capacity (gallons) _____ Quick recovery? Brand name _____

5. Exterior sillcocks (faucets)? Frost free?

Heating

1. Furnace capacity (BTUs) _____ fuel _____ brand name _____

2. Number of electric baseboard units _____ wattage per unit _____ brand name _____

or

Number of hot-water baseboard units _____ material _____ brand name _____

or

Hot-air ducts material _____

3. Number of thermostats _____ locations _____

4. Number of heating zones (for hot water or hot air heat only) _____ which rooms are in which zones _____

Electricity

1. Current (amperes) _____

2. Circuit breaker or fuse box?

3. Wiring size _____ grade _____ capacity _____

4. Number of outlets per room _____ Grounded outlets (three-prong)? Safety type?

5. Exterior outlets _____ location _____

6. Switches per room _____ location _____ type _____

7. Interior lighting fixtures (describe) _____

8. Exterior lighting fixtures (describe) _____

Bathroom Appliances and Fixtures

1. Bathroom sink type _____ size _____ material _____ brand name _____

2. Bathtub length _____ depth _____ material _____ brand name _____

3. Toilet type _____ material _____ brand name _____

4. Medicine cabinet size _____ mirror? Electric outlet? Light?

5. Accessories: Soap dish at sink? Soap dish at bathtub? Toilet paper dispenser? Shower curtain rod? Shower door? Shower door material _____ Shower door dimension _____ Towel rods? Toothbrush holder? Other _____

Kitchen Appliances and Fixtures

1. Kitchen sink size _____ Single bowl? Double bowl? Material _____ brand name _____

2. Refrigerator type _____ capacity (in cubic feet) _____ Frost free?

3. Stove type: Electric? Gas? Eye-level oven? Width _____ brand name _____

4. Dishwasher type _____ interior lining material _____ capacity _____ brand name _____

Utility Room Appliances and Fixtures

1. Clothes washer capacity (in pounds) _____ interior lining material _____ brand name _____

2. Clothes dryer capacity (in pounds) _____ interior lining material _____ brand name _____

3. Utility sink type _____ size _____ material _____ brand name _____ Plumbing supplied?

Fireplace

1. Working fireplace or decorative only?

2. Freestanding working fireplace? Built-in fireplace? Size of hearth _____ Fireplace material _____ Mantel for built-in fireplace? Heatolator for built-in fireplace?

Furnishings

Buyers of mobile homes will find that furnishings are or can be provided by the unit manufacturer. Occasionally modular home manufacturers will offer furnishing or "decor" packages.

1. Number and type of kitchen furniture provided _____ sizes _____ brand names _____ other descriptions _____

2. Number and type of dining room furniture provided _____ sizes _____ brand names _____ other descriptions _____

3. Number and type of living room furniture provided _____ sizes _____ brand names _____ other descriptions _____

4. Number and type of bedroom furniture provided _____ sizes _____ brand names _____ other descriptions _____

5. Number and type of furniture provided for other rooms _____ sizes _____ brand names _____ other descriptions _____

6. Type, fabric, length, and other details of drapes or curtains in kitchen _____

7. Type, fabric, length, and other details of drapes or curtains in dining room _____

8. Type, fabric, length, and other details of drapes or curtains in living room _____

9. Type, fabric, length, and other details of drapes or curtains in bedrooms _____

10. Type, fabric, length, and other details of drapes or curtains in other rooms _____

11. Miscellaneous decorative accessories in kitchen (describe) _____

12. Miscellaneous decorative accessories in dining room (describe) _____

13. Miscellaneous decorative accessories in living room (describe) _____

14. Miscellaneous decorative accessories in bedrooms (describe) _____

15. Miscellaneous decorative accessories in other rooms (describe) _____

Air Conditioning

1. Central air conditioning? Individual room units? Adequate wiring to accommodate air conditioning?

2. Type of unit _____ cooling capacity (BTU/hour) _____

For those who would like an even more detailed specifications list, write to the Farmers Home Administration office in your community or in Washington D.C. and request a copy of *Dwelling Specifications*.

BIBLIOGRAPHY

Anderson, L. O. *How to Build a Wood Frame House.* New York: Dover Publications, Inc., 1973. Also available from the Government Printing Office in Washington, D.C., as *Wood Frame House Construction* (Agricultural Handbook #73, 1970). This book deals only with construction aspects in a thorough and clear fashion, with many good diagrams. Mechanical systems are not covered.

Blackburn, Graham. *Illustrated Housebuilding.* Woodstock, N.Y.: Overlook Press, 1974. Fun to read if you don't mind plowing through a handwritten text. The book covers the basics of building a frame house, including information on mechanical systems. Aimed at the do-it-yourselfer, it does provide an understanding of how a house is built; a conventional house, that is.

Blue Book. This book gives values of used mobile homes. It is available from Judy Berner Publishing Co., 10060 West Roosevelt Road, Westchester, Illinois 60153.

Boudreau, Eugene. *Buying Country Land.* New York: Macmillan, 1973 (paperback). The author is a geologist and the emphasis in the book reflects this bias. The book offers a very detailed discussion of ground water and percolation tests but is thin on the legal aspects of land purchase. We recommend the book if you are buying land which will require a well and septic system.

Center for Auto Safety. *Mobile Homes: The Low Cost Housing Hoax.* New York: Grossman Publishers, 1975. This has been described as an "exposé of the mobile home industry." The Center for Auto Safety was founded by Ralph Nader. The book deals with problems of safety, construction quality, mobile park rules, dealers and financing, and is well worth reading if you are considering a mobile home. Bear in mind that Nader's "raiders" have often been accused—by those who are being exposed—of seeing things at their blackest and for reaching conclusions on the basis of cursory research.

Dietz, Albert. *Dwelling House Construction.* Cambridge, Mass.: The M.I.T. Press, 1946, rev. ed. 1971. This is an excellent book, very detailed and technical. Many older construction techniques that are more elaborate than those used currently are discussed. The book deals only with construction and site work and does not cover mechanical systems. Many diagrams; a fine reference book.

Domebook Two. Available from Pacific Domes (a manufacturer), Box 279, Bolinas, California 94924. A "counter-culture" book which presents the experiences of people who have built domes, with some useful information about particular features of domes—doors, windows, sealing, etc.

FHA Regulations. Contact your local office of FHA and also VA for their regulations and whatever lists they might have of approved mobile, modular, and prefabricated housing manufacturers.

Griffin, Al. *So You Want to Buy a Mobile Home*. New York: Pocket Books, 1972 (paperback). The author takes a generally favorable approach to mobile homes and offers useful information about construction, equipment, and standards as well as a list of manfacturers.

House & Home Directory of Modular Housing Producers. This book is published annually by House & Home, 1221 Avenue of the Americas, New York, New York 10020. Though it is published primarily to assist builders of subdivisions and suppliers to the modular housing industry, it is also useful for the consumer. It lists manufacturers alphabetically and by state.

Manufactured Housing Association of America. *Mobile and Modular Home Directory*. This is the annual publication of the association. The directory is devoted primarily to mobile homes, though a few modular homes are represented. Manufacturers pay for the right to appear in the publication, which is available from Hanley Publishing Company, Inc., 1718 Sherman Avenue, Evanston, Illinois 60201.

Mobile Homes Manufacturers Association. MHMA, 14560 Lee Road, Chantilly, Virginia, 22021, will send you their brochure "Mobile Housing Publications" and a price list. Among the most useful publications are *Standard for Mobile Homes* [ANSI (American National Standards Institute) A 119.1], *Standard for Mobile Home Parks, Owner's Guide to Mobile Home Maintenance,* and *Tips on Buying a Mobile Home*. Bear in mind that this is the industry's organ. MHMA also publishes a list of publications about mobile homes available from extension services of various state universities.

Moral, Herbert R. *Buying Country Property*. Charlotte, Vt.: Garden Way Publishing Co., 1972. Some useful information on how to think about the kind of land you want and whether that land might be farmed.

Murray, Robert W., Jr. *How to Buy the Right House at the Right Price*. New York: Macmillan, 1971. (paperback). Useful information about floor plans, mechanical systems, and construction.

National Association of Building Manufacturers. *Builder's Guide to Manufactured Homes*. This is the annual publication, in magazine format, of the Association (1619 Massachusetts Avenue, N. W., Washington, D.C. 20036). It contains articles plus a membership list (many firms might not belong to the NABM) including modular and prefabricated housing manufacturers, with information on shipping area, types of homes sold, and whether catalogs are available.

Oliver, Craig S. "Landscaping the Mobile Home." University Park, Pa.: Pennsylvania State University, College of Agriculture Extension Service, n.d. Sections of this 4-page pamphlet have been reprinted in this book, in the mobile home chapter, but it is well worth having if you are planning a single-story, rectangular mobile, modular, or prefabricated home.

Prenis, John, ed. *The Dome Builder's Handbook*. Philadelphia: Running Press, 1974. A first-hand account of building "every kind of dome" from scratch. Not especially useful if you are buying a kit.

Price, Irving. *Buying Country Property*. New York: Pyramid Communications, Inc., 1974 (paperback). The author is a real estate broker and his emphasis is on legal and financial aspects of land transfer. He does offer some useful advice on selecting the location of land for a home.

Roberts, Rex. *Your Engineered House*. Philadelphia: Lippincott, 1964. Fun to read. Basic things to think about when you design your own home and useful when considering a manufactured home that allows some custom design.

Wason, Betty. *It Takes "Jack" To Build a House.* New York: St. Martin's Press, 1968. A first-person account of helping to build a house. The homeowner-builder relationship is explored in great detail (the builder comes off a very poor second). It could be subtitled "a book of pitfalls" and might well dampen your enthusiasm for the whole project. Useful diagrams and hints.

Watkins, A. M. *Building or Buying the High Quality House at Lowest Cost.* Garden City, N.Y.: Doubleday, 1962 (paperback). A general discussion of what to consider when buying a house; good discussion of mechanical systems.

Woodall's Mobile Home and Park Directory. This annual publication of Woodall Publishing Company, 500 Hyacinth Place, Highland Park, Illinois 60035, is invaluable for choosing a mobile home community. In addition to articles about mobile home living, all of which are positive in tone, there are advertisements of manufacturers plus a listing of mobile home parks by state and locality, giving type, size, community facilities, and a rating of from one to five stars based on explained criteria. The Center for Auto Safety book mentioned above discusses Woodall's criteria.

Codes

Here are the principal codes that manufacturers may refer to in their literature. They will say that they subscribe to the code or are members of the organization. Reading the codes, many of which might be readily available at your public library, will tell you exactly how useful it is to know whether a unit is built to one or another of the codes.

American National Standards Institute (ANSI-A 119.1) is available from Mobile Homes Manufacturers Association, 14560 Lee Road, Chantilly, Virginia 22021.

The BOCA Basic Building Code is available from Building Officials and Code Administrators International, 1313 East 60th Street, Chicago, Illinois 60637.

The ICBO Uniform Building Code is available from International Conference of Building Officials, 50 South Robles, Pasadena, California 91101.

The National Building Code is available from the American Insurance Association, Engineering and Safety Department, 85 John Street, New York, New York 10038.

The Southern Standard Building Code is available from Southern Building Code Congress, International Conference of Building Officials (ICBO), 50 South Robles, Pasadena, California 91101.

INDEX

(Page numbers in italics refer to illustrations.)